Great Smoky Mountains

MW00680975

Great Smoky Mountains
National Park
North Carolina and Tennessee

Produced by the
Division of Publications
National Park Service

U.S. Department of the Interior
Washington, D.C. 1981

The National Park Handbook Series
National Park Handbooks, compact introductions to
the great natural and historic places administered by
the National Park Service, are designed to promote
understanding and enjoyment of the parks. Each is in-
tended to be informative reading and a useful guide
before, during, and after a park visit. More than 100
titles are in print. This is Handbook 112. You may
purchase the handbooks through the mail by writing to
Superintendent of Documents, U.S. Government Print-
ing Office, Washington, DC 20402.

About This Book
Great Smoky Mountains National Park straddles the
North Carolina-Tennessee border and encompasses the
climax of the Appalachian Mountain System. Major attractions are the mountains themselves, the preserved
structures and lore of mountain folklife, stupendous displays of flowering plants and shrubs, fall colors, wild
animals, superb hiking opportunities, and gorgeous
rivers, streams, and waterfalls. This handbook is published in support of the National Park Service's management policies and interpretive programs at the park.
Part 1 gives a brief introduction to what you may find
in a leisurely visit to the park; Part 2 outlines the natural
history of the mountains and their valleys; and Part 3
presents concise travel guide and reference materials.

Library of Congress Cataloging in Publication Data
United States.   National Park Service.
Great Smoky Mountains National Park, North
Carolina and Tennessee.
(National park handbook; 112)
Includes index.
1. Great Smoky Mountains National Park (N.C. and
Tenn.) I. Title. II. Series: Handbook (United States.
National Park Service. Division of Publications); 112.
F443.G7U63   1981   976.8'89   81-11320
                          AACR2

Contents

Welcome to the Great Smokies

The Appalachians at Their Best

At first glimpse there appear to be two Smokies: the mountains' wild nature, and the folk life. The mind calls up both the sweeping mountain vistas whose peaks succeed peaks to the far horizon and the rustic cabins and barns set off with the split rail fences of 19th-century mountain life. The mountains are everywhere, punctuated by restored settlements, by Cades Cove, Mingus Mill, Cataloochee, and Little Greenbrier. But this is not the full story for there are many, many Great Smokies, a double fistful of which may be just for you. There are as many Great Smokies as there are people who come here intent on discovering their secrets: the folklorist's and amateur historian's Smokies; the trout angler's Smokies; the Smokies of the backpacker, day-tripper, and trail walker; the botanist's, ecologist's, and birder's Smokies; and the automobile tourist's Smokies. Take your pick.

You can walk into the Smokies, into the heart of the wilderness. You can drive through the Smokies, through the jewels in the crown of the Appalachian highlands. You can enter them through North Carolina or through Tennessee. But you can also enter them through any strong interest *you* may have, for there are as many Smokies as there are ways you can see them. And one good way to see them is through the eyes of a native son whose love for these mountains is exceeded only by his love for people. Such is Glenn Cardwell.

Glenn Cardwell took his aging mother and father down to the Noah "Bud" Ogle cabin just after the National Park Service finished restoring it. Glenn works for the park and would conduct nature walks at the cabin, so he wanted to see what his folks would say. They used to live nearby and his mother's Aunt Cindy and her husband, Noah, built the cabin just off Cherokee Orchard Road out of Gatlinburg.

"Well I'll tell you," Glenn said, "my mother got to reminiscing not one step off the parking lot and stopped at every rock and spot in the yard and told a tale. It must've taken the better part of an hour just to get her through the yard and down to the porch."

Glenn's mother took one look at the porch and said, "They put the step [a big flat rock] in the wrong place." And so the restoration team had . . . but it was another

Here in the East's wettest corner, winter snows release moisture slowly into the ground until spring thaw swells streams to rush downslope. The ultimate destination? The Gulf of Mexico. Preceding pages: A rustic Cades Cove cabin preserves the spirit of pioneer life and times. Cover photo: Sunrise from Mt. LeConte, Great Smoky Mountains National Park.

rock that bothered Mrs. Cardwell most.

Walking back to the car she stopped dead in her tracks and said despairingly, "What have they *done* to Cindy's rock?"

Glenn had no idea what she meant although he could see the road cut close to a big boulder. The road had been relocated but Glenn recalled nothing unusual about the rock.

His mother, still staring, repeated her question. Glenn's father shrugged, "Looks to me like somebody blowed hell out of it."

"I still couldn't figure out what was bothering my mother," Glenn said.

But now, in the 1980s, he will tell you that everyone in the Smokies had scaffolds in their yards back in Aunt Cindy's day for drying fruits and vegetables for winter storage. Everyone, that is, but Aunt Cindy. She used the big boulder across from their cabin, or what used to be the flat part of it. Many's the time Glenn's mother, as a little girl, helped Aunt Cindy spread produce to sun dry on the rock.

Glenn Cardwell is an affable walking encyclopedia of Smokies life at the time the Smokies changed from a piece of Tennessee and North Carolina real estate into our second national park in the East. Stories such as Glenn's—and there are many—supply a compelling human resonance to this wilderness land. Glenn's enthusiasm is a bit unusual, because his father was bought out *twice* by the Federal government as lands were being acquired for the park. And each buy-out meant an unplanned relocation for the family, moving and building anew.

"I think if my mother hadn't had me on the way at the time of the first buy-out," Glenn said, "my father would have pulled up stakes and gone back to Cumberland, Virginia, like many, many of our other relatives did." But the Cardwells stayed on near the park and Glenn embodies a transition, bridging new and old ways of doing and seeing things here. His father was bitter at first, but when he visited the Noah "Bud" Ogle Cabin years later he admitted he was glad the park had come along so that some things remained unchanged. It was nice, he said, that he and others could still see the land as it had been.

The Great Smokies represented a new direction in national park policy in the 1920s. The eighteen national parks then in existence in the West had been created from lands already owned by the Federal government. The Smokies lands authorized for park purchase beginning in 1926 were all in private ownership in more than 6,600 tracts. The lion's share was owned by eighteen timber and pulpwood companies, but 1,200 other tracts were farms. Worse, there were also more than 5,000 lots and summer homes. Many of these had been won in promotion schemes and their owners had never bothered to pay taxes on them. This created an awesome land acquisition headache.

The Federal government would not purchase land for national parks in those days, so in 1927 the Tennessee and North Carolina legislatures each provided for appropriation of $2 million to purchase the land. Already, $1 million had been pledged. The legislation also created State Park Commissions in each state to handle the buying. The John D. Rockefeller family supplemented the fund drive with a $5 million donation. This was considered one of the biggest and most important accomplishments of the entire national park movement. The two states eventually purchased the needed lands and donated them to the Federal government.

Ten years of dogged, full-scale activity and several more years of tying up loose ends were required to get the acquisition job done. Despite this tremendous impact of human land use in the Smokies, however, about forty percent of the park's 209,000 hectares (517,000 acres) constitutes the East's most extensive virgin forest. Forest recovery is now well underway throughout the park despite the former blight left by logging and subsequent forest fires, and landslides, and other forms of erosion.

At one time no sharp edge separated two aspects of nature in the Great Smokies: man and the wilderness. Cherokee Indians lived here in ways ironically similar to those of the whites who would soon displace them. They cultivated crops, hunted, believed in one god, practiced a democratic form of government, and lived not in teepees but in mud-and-log structures. "The place of blue smoke," *Shaconage*, they called this mountain hunting ground. And here amidst the haze lived also the spirit of their people; it, too, could not be divorced from the land itself. Treaty after treaty saw the Cherokees lose more and more homeland, up to and finally including the Smokies. In one of the great human tragedies that blots American history they were forcibly removed westward, "relocated" to Oklahoma via the "Trail of Tears." One fourth of the people died along the way. A few Cherokees had resisted removal, staying behind in small groups and hiding out in the mountains. Troops could not relocate

Next two pages: A contented cow lends realism to the reconstructed Pioneer Farmstead, next to Oconaluftee Visitor Center. Pages 12-13: Mt. LeConte is the park's third highest peak, following Mt. Guyot and Clingmans Dome, the highest. Smokies rocks are among the continent's oldest sediments. The ranges have survived 200 million years of erosion. By contrast, the Sierra Nevada is thought to be only 1 million years old.

them because they couldn't *locate* them. Later the Cherokees were allowed to return and reclaim the borders of their old homeland. They live there today on the Cherokee Reservation.

It is difficult now to appreciate the pressure once exerted on the Appalachian highlands by human settlement. Back when land meant livelihood to a nation of agrarian people, the gradual pressure from the eastern coast, across the Piedmont, reached the Appalachian chain. The shortage of arable lands forced people into and finally onto the mountains in search of a plot of ground that would produce a livelihood. And so settlement came to the Great Smokies, gradually working its way up the mountainsides to the limits of cultivation. Grazing was eventually pushed beyond those limits all the way up the mountain to the balds. Combined overgrazing, overfishing, destructive logging practices, and overhunting would soon turn dense wilderness into a ravaged landscape. The National Park was authorized in 1926, established for protection in 1930, and established for development in 1934. And now, about 50 years later, wilderness is again in ascendancy, as field naturalist Napier Shelton amply testifies as he takes you exploring in Part Two of this handbook.

The wilderness richness here is both astounding and close at hand. Richness? There are more species of salamanders here—22—than in any other part of the world. In the lush density of the Smokies forests there are more tree species than in all of Northern Europe. It is thought that this sheer density of forest cover and its attendant transpiration help account for the "misty" character for which the Great Smoky Mountains are named.

This forest richness continues to unfold for present-day biologists, as the recent discovery of the paper birch in the Smokies attests. It had long been held that this northern species did not occur in Tennessee. Its range generally swings southward into New Jersey and then simply jumps along the Appalachians, appearing here and there as elevation and other conditions simulate northerly climes.

Peter White, plant ecologist with the National Park Service's Uplands Biological Field Research Laboratory in the Smokies, discovered several of the trees one day when he went out to verify a paper birch sighted by three North Carolina graduate students two years before. "It was located on a manway or unmaintained trail," White said, "right on the trail, one of the steepest in the park. So if you knew what you were looking for there was no missing it. Actually what we have here in the Smokies is called the mountain paper birch, which may or may not be a different species than the classic white birch which would be called the true or typical paper birch."

White is fascinated with unusual plant occurrences. A major passion of his here in the Smokies is to track down the mystery of the circumpolar twinflower, *Linnaea*, collected from "the mountains of Sevier County in Tennessee" by amateur botanist Albert Ruth in 1891. This is the only report of the plant south of certain bogs in West Virginia, and White hopes to verify it.

"Ruth misidentified this *Linnaea* as partridgeberry and it wasn't known about until 1934, when it came to the University of Tennessee with the Ruth Collection from Texas," White said. "Jack Sharp at the university recognized its true identity and its significance."

The Ruth Collection came to Tennessee because the university's plant herbarium was destroyed by fire in the 1920s and the university sought to build it up again. The twinflower was discovered by the great botanist Carl Linnaeus in Finland and named for him by a friend. It occurs from Eurasia to North America as a northern species, hence the "circumpolar" description.

"There are pluses and minuses to believing the plant came from here," White explained. "Ruth was a careful field botanist with a good eye, and many plants are named for him. He collected many species for the first time. But we also know from his collections that some of his labels are vague."

White's quest for the elusive twinflower growing far south of its normal range symbolizes an aspect of the Smokies. The park has been designated an International Biosphere Reserve. As one writer put it: All the world of ecology comes to the Great Smokies . . . Scientists and students come to observe the richness and density of life forms; the misplaced species; the dramatic impacts of catastrophic landslides and fire scars; and the unknowns, those tantalizing areas of knowledge still withholding their secrets despite careful scrutiny. What really happened here during the glacial periods? Where were the trees then? How much forest burning did Cherokees use for game and vegetation management purposes before Europeans came? Speculations aside, what is the true story behind grassy balds? What are the seasonal migration patterns of the juncos that stay in the park year-round? These remain questions stirring the expert

Next two pages: Abundant cascades and inviting waterfalls greet you in the Smokies. Their sprays often water luxuriant mosses and make ideal habitat for the Smokies' surprising number of salamanders and aquatic insects.

and amateur alike to earnest inquiry.

Perhaps you may come to make one of these questions your own. Nature, it turns out, is an unfolding process. It is a continuous coping, albeit gradual, with change, so that our knowledge always remains limited and there is ever much more to learn. If you have questions, do feel free to ask them. Ask them of a ranger, a naturalist, or the people behind the counters at the visitor centers. But the more closely you observe the nature of things here in the Smokies, the more likely your questions will be to draw a blank. Don't be disappointed by this. Be encouraged: your question without an answer, should you pursue it, might hold the key to understanding some facet of the natural world tomorrow. But you will have to look at the Smokies, really look with honest and inquiring eyes, to stump the likes of Glenn Cardwell and Peter White or any number of other people you might meet here in the park.

All questions aside, however, one thing is certain: millions have come here in pursuit of recreation and gone away fully satisfied, to return again and again. Great Smoky Mountains National Park is a great place to *do* things, things we describe in Part Three of this handbook, your "Guide and Adviser." May *you* return again and again.

Don't let the glorious mountain vistas distract you from the beauty at your feet. The park boasts more than 2,000 species of mushrooms. They are conspicuous because abundant moisture may encourage them to fruit several times a year.

The Nature of Things
In the Highlands

A One-day Walk to Maine

Every spring a number of enterprising people set out to walk more than 3,000 kilometers (2,000 miles) on the Appalachian Trail from Georgia to Maine. Those who finish typically arrive some four months later. You can experience nearly the same thing—in terms of the natural history and particularly forest cover—in a single day by hiking from the lowlands to the crest of the Smokies. Because of the climatic change accompanying this gain in altitude, as much as 1,500 meters (5,000 feet), such a walk can take you, as it were, through the oak and pine forests of northern Georgia, the oak-hickory forests of central Virginia, the northern hardwoods of Massachusetts, and into the spruce-fir forests of Maine and Canada. And along the way you get many glimpses of the natural processes that shape and control the national park's marvelous assemblage of life.

If you're not quite ready for such a long, hard climb, why not join me for an armchair ascent of the mountains?

It's early on a summer morning and the sky is clear, but knowing the frequency of rain in the Smokies, we tuck ponchos into our packs. As our boots crunch pleasantly on the gravel of an old mountain road, we listen to the neighboring stream and look at the forested hollow it drains. Just a few decades ago farm children played in the stream, and cornfields bordered the road. Now we can enjoy the stream in the shade of yellow-poplar trees that now stand thick and straight where the grain once did.

Around a bend the stream gradient steepens and so does the road. We are still in young forest; here it grows where cattle formerly grazed or lumbermen felled its giant ancestors. For some time we labor upwards, the road becoming a trail and a few big trees appearing along the tumbling creek. Then, rather suddenly, there is a striking difference in the environment. We have crossed the line into primeval forest, into territory where the axman has not been and most of the trees are big. This is Great Smokies virgin cove forest, a type unrivaled in the northern hemisphere for combined variety and size of trees. Here it is cool, shady, and moist. The tree trunks shoot high above into the canopy, which intercepts most

For sheer numbers and diversity of trees and flowering plants, the park is a botanical showplace. Its varied elevations telescope together nearly all forest types found from Maine to Georgia. Hiker and motorist alike may see wildflowers from March through October. Preceding pages: Common wood sorrel blooms in forest shade in spring and summer, depending on elevation. One flowering shrub, the witch hazel, blooms in fall and early winter.

of the sunlight and seems to enclose us in a private world. The ground around us is covered with the greenery of small plants. We hear bird songs but cannot see the singers.

The peace and grandeur of the forest are interrupted by a slight movement off to our right. In the leaves beneath a large, rotting log a tiny shrew restlessly sniffs with its long nose. It moves in short thrusts through the dead leaves, searching with a fierce intensity for worms, crickets, or any animal small enough to overcome. Impelled by hunger, this normally nocturnal animal has been emboldened by the shadiness to venture into the cove forest's subdued daylight. The shrew is just one infinitesimal part of the great forest, in which thousands of living things seek the energy and nutrients needed for survival. The shrew hunts, as it were, a fragment of the sun's energy, transmitted through plants and then through the small plant-eating creatures that it preys upon.

Crossing a log bridge below a waterfall, we see fish darting under boulders. Spray from the falls drifts over us and onto the dark thickets of rhododendron crowding the stream banks. We try to keep the cool water in our minds as we start up the long switchbacks ascending the valley's south-facing slope. Trees of the cove forest, buckeye, hemlock, sugar maple, and their many associates, gradually become scarcer, and oaks and hickories become the dominant trees. Halfway up the slope we have climbed from coolness into warmth. Here in the more open oak forest, the sun beams down through the foliage, heating the ground and air.

A few gulps from the canteen and we can face the last switchbacks up the slope and onto a sunstruck, rocky ridge. The sun has real authority here. Winding more gradually upward along this ridge, the trail now takes us beneath pines, trees that are adapted to such hot, dry situations. If it weren't for the trail, we would have a tough time making our way through the thickets of mountain-laurel spread beneath the scattered pines. A towhee, lover of such thickets, calls its name as we pass. In one stretch we go through a brown patch of dead pines. After several mild winters, southern pine beetles have multiplied and feasted here. If the next winter is not cold enough to kill most of the beetle larvae, the patch of dead pines may increase greatly in size.

The trail now slants off onto the north side of the ridge. Right away the air is somewhat cooler here where part of the day the ridgetop shields it from the sun. The pines quickly disappear, and beeches, yellow birches, maples, and buckeyes form the forest. You New Englanders should now feel quite at home, among these tree species that accompany us all the way across the mountain's north and east flank. Then, as we approach the 1,500-meter (5,000-foot) level, the dark spires of scattered spruces begin to appear, signaling the nearness of the Smokies' crowning forest.

But before we make the final ascent, let's take a short detour to a nearby knob, which promises a spectacular view, a welcome visual release after being shut in so long by foliage. Going up the side of the knob, we quickly leave the forest and begin tunneling through dense thickets of rhododendron and mountain-laurel. Trees don't grow here at all. On top, the shrubs become smaller and we can look out over them. Perched on the end of a spur from the side of a giant valley, we look up to high ridges on both sides and down to a stream far below. Is it our imagination, or do we really hear that stream whispering to us of the humid, secret world way down there under the big trees? For many minutes we are lost in contemplation of the Smokies' green-blue spaces.

The crack of thunder suddenly wakens us from our reverie. A bank of clouds, dark underneath and contorted with churning air, is rolling over the ridges and into the head of the valley. The clouds shoot lightning toward the slopes below. Hypnotized by the spectacle we remain rooted to our rocks until the first drops fall, then we pull on our ponchos, determined to greet the storm. Soon the valley view is blotted out by boiling clouds. We and a circle of shrubs, both whipped by rain and wind, are all that exist in the world. Our foolhardiness on this exposed knob is soon revealed as lightning flashes so near that its crackling sound is almost instantaneous. We hurry down the trail, now a small torrent where it tunnels through the rhododendrons, and in a few minutes we reach safer ground. We eat our lunch under sheltering hemlocks. When we sense the end of the storm, we head toward our day's goal, the top of the Smokies. The deciduous forest rapidly turns into a coniferous one, the beech, birch, maple, buckeye, and others giving way to a nearly solid stand of spruce and fir. This is an enchanted forest. Carpets of mosses and ferns, struggling, as it were, for growing space, make delicate patterns on the forest floor. Limber-stemmed shrubs lift round or toothed leaves to the pale, post-storm light filtering through the thick evergreen foliage of the trees above. Out of the stillness, like the voice of some tiny fairy, comes the tinkling medley of a winter wren. We stop and listen. We watch a drop of water fall from the tip of a fern. We feel the coolness, a coolness born of altitude. We have reached Maine right here in the Smokies.

A short distance beyond, the trail breaks out onto the top of a cliff, opening to us the whole breadth of the mountains. This is our final reward; and as we sit here we see, without knowing it, a summary of our day's experience. We see landslide scars on the mountainside that probably came during a storm like the one we just experienced, when the earth, heavy with water and lying thinly over the smooth rock beneath, could no longer hang on and slipped in a crashing avalanche down the slope; like the pine beetle, landslides are one of the many natural forces that challenge the forest's powers of recuperation. Chimney swifts pick insects from the air and we hear the chatter of a red squirrel interrupted in its hunt for cones. Like the shrew, each in its own special way is busy gaining the fuel to stay alive. Each, through its interaction with plants and animals, affects the total fabric of Smokies life. Far below, the trees of a cove forest march up a stream valley; on the slopes above them spreads a mantle of oaks. A narrow ridge far down and off to the right bears the dark green of pines. Nearer, we see the ragged lower edge of the spruce-fir forest, where it fingers into the northern hardwoods below it. But we sense an overall unity because each kind of forest merges into the next, creating an unbroken mantle that lies over all the ridges as far as the eye can see.

There is no true alpine tundra in the Smokies, such as we might find atop certain mountains in New York and New England and atop many mountains in the West. But alpine experiences aplenty await us here for the climbing. They can be had on ridges, peaks, and, even pinnacles, from atop which we gaze out over a forested sea of peaks. It is a rare reminder of the mantle of forest that once lay unbroken over the eastern United States. It is often said that when Europeans first encountered America, a squirrel could walk from the Atlantic Ocean to the Mississippi without touching the ground!

Clouds drift over the mountain waves. Like the clouds of many yesterdays, they have dropped their burden of excess moisture on the forests, maintaining the wetness that encourages the lush plant growth of the Smokies. Then, through a break in the clouds, the sun finally shines, sending renewed charges of energy into the forest and ultimately through all the life of the forest. Much of the pattern of forest types is determined by the way the sun's rays strike the mountain slopes. Through changes in its daily duration and height in the sky the sun makes the seasons. Through its powers to evaporate ocean water and provide the energy that moves air, it can even be said to bring the rain itself.

Georgia to Maine, Straight Up

A hike from Cades Cove to Clingmans Dome simulates walking from North Georgia to Maine. You will begin in Cades Cove amidst oak and pine forests which also grow in northern Georgia. Your walk will end atop Clingmans Dome in spruce-fir forests characteristic of Maine and Canada. In between you will hike beneath the canopies of oak-hickory-red maple forests that characterize Virginia, and the northern hardwoods of Massachusetts. The reason for this localized insight into the whole of the eastern United States forest types is the vertical rise of the Great Smoky Mountains. The Smokies' highest peaks stand 1,500 meters (5,000 feet) above its lowlands.

The axiom is this: here in the Smokies, elevation gain simulates a shift to more northerly latitudes. Of course, this is a generalization. On an actual hike from Cades Cove to Clingmans Dome you would have to detour a lot to take in all the variety of eastern U.S. forest types. But all except true alpine tundra are here, although not laid out in a straight line.

In rough attempts to measure the Smokies' *local* climates, the rule of thumb is that spring advances up the mountains. At lower elevations, for example, spring beauty blooms by early March. At 1,500 meters (5,000 feet) elevation, however, it may still be in full bloom two to three months later.

Remarkably, the Smokies provide a plant laboratory encompassing most of the eastern U.S. major forest vegetation types. This, and the fact that virgin forests are rare in the East, make it no wonder that the Great Smoky Mountains National Park has been designated an International Biosphere Reserve.

This international recognition of and commitment to preserving the Smokies underscores the park's wealth of natural history.

You need not be an expert to observe this. Sharp eyes and curiosity will in themselves unfold great portions of this natural history lore for you to ponder.

In the first low reaches of your one-day trip from Georgia to Maine here in the Smokies, crossvine, grapevine, or lady's-slipper (photo) may be blooming. These flowers, like the Virginia, pitch, and shortleaf pines,

cling to the warmest local climates. They also follow the driest slopes and ridges only part way up the mountains. As you gain elevation you quickly leave these species behind.

The contrast between your lowlands trailhead and the 1,800-meter (6,000-foot) summit is amazing. Even the chickadees change en route. The Carolina species holds forth down here in the cove, but gives way to the black-capped chickadee some-

where around 1,500 meters (5,000 feet). The fence lizard is a dry, pine woods creature. Like the Carolina chickadee, it generally avoids higher elevations.

Each animal and plant drops out at a different limit as you gain altitude, but more than half of your journey will be through deciduous forest, of the cove hardwood type or oak woodland. Smokies forests are rich: there are more tree species here than in all of Northern Europe.

As you travel the lower forests you will probably hear the songs of the ovenbird, wood thrush, and pileated woodpecker, birds you would hear in mature timber throughout the eastern United States. The gray squirrel and the box turtle (bottom photo), both familiar creatures, will be occasional trailside companions in these broad-leaved woodlands. The basswood tree (top photo) is considered an "indicator" of the cove hardwood forest type. The magnolias, with their oversize leaves, catch the eye of most people traveling south from, say, Pennsylvania,

when they hit the Smokies. Almost a natural "cultural shock," these trees announce that you have arrived in a different place. Magnificent magnolias appear along the trail, thinning in number and decreasing in size as soon as you leave the cove.

32

Along streams and on the shaded slopes below 1,220 meters (4,000 feet), look for rosebay rhododendron (top photo), yellow buckeye (bottom right photo), basswood, yellow-poplar, and other cove hardwood "indicator" species. They signal that you still have a ways to go in your day's climb. On the cove forest floor in spring you may be lucky enough to spot the great white trillium (immediate right photo). It was popular after the Civil War for decorating graves and so has become, in many places, a scarce plant because of this practice. It is protected here in the national park, as are all plants, animals, historic structures, and archeological artifacts. Please respect these—and the right of others who follow you to enjoy them in their natural or historical setting.

The red squirrel's raucous chatter—you can't believe such a small creature makes such a big racket—tells you that you are leaving the cove forest. The "boomer," as it is known locally, will likely announce your presence periodically to the whole forest from here clear to the top of the mountain. Farther north these red squirrels may be called pine squirrels; out west, chickarees. Some would argue over the species involved, but not over the noise they make!

The songs of the winter wren and veery, a thrush, also signal that you have climbed above the cove now. But the northern bird of the mountains that excites us here is the raven. This resourceful bird, often mistaken for the smaller crow, eats anything small enough and drives away anything that's too big to eat. That's an exaggeration, but ravens are contemptuous even of hawks aloft in the same windstream.

The spruce trees announce that you have gotten to Maine at last! The blackish coloration of spruce forests reaching here and there down off the crests of the Smokies is conspicuous in all seasons. It is from this coloration of spruce stands that the nearby Black Mountains of North Carolina are named. The spruce-fir forest is a product of winter cold and summer rain in such a combination that prevents their invasion by deciduous trees just down-slope.

Cove Hardwood Forest

A degree of romance or mystique surrounds the cove hardwood forest. The name was used as early as 1905 in professional forestry literature, but was probably coined much earlier, perhaps in the days of settlement.

The coves share all of their predominant trees with the neighboring plant communities, and no common animal or plant is restricted to cove forest. The key to its recognition is *variety,* particularly in the make-up of the canopy, the name given to the roof level of any woodland. Cove forest is not restricted literally to topographic flats and hollows; it may also occur on steep slopes, where soil moisture conditions are suitable.

In its best development, cove forest may sustain 20-25 tree species tangling branches far overhead. Look for white ash, sugar maple, magnolia, American beech, silverbell, and basswood. If most of these are present, with or without buckeye, holly, yellow birch, and hemlock, you are being treated to cove hardwood scenery.

Oaks, hickories, red maple and yellow-poplar (tulip tree) will also be present, but these widespread species are not really useful in settling the question. One often workable rule of thumb is the presence of yellow-wood, but this small tree is absent from the cove hardwood forest community in many parts of the park.

Many of today's typical cove hardwood trees have also been found as fossils in rocks of Cretaceous age in the eastern United States. This match up— and the recognition that the southern mountains have been continuously available for land plant growth since Dinosaur Days—has given plant geographers much food for thought. Cove forest is now plausibly regarded as a very ancient mixture of species. Probably, it was the ancestor of several other widespread forest communities. Perhaps it was the haven of refuge sought by many plants and animals during the Pleistocene glacial period. Its significance today is its wealth of species composition and its heritage—millions of years of forest evolution. We are fortunate that significant stands of this forest type survive uncut in the Great Smoky Mountains.

A great benefit of these rich, lush forests for hikers is the refreshing coolness they afford on hot summer days. Many people have described them as "green cathedrals" because of the coolness, rest, and peace they seem to engender.

When the yellow-poplar seeds into an abandoned farm field it means that the field could eventually become a cove forest. But the yellow-poplar needs the company of a dozen other species to form true cove forest.

The yellow-poplar grows fast and straight. Its bark has white-sided ridges.

Cove forest has less moss cover than the spruce-fir forest, but it boasts more kinds of mosses. The abundance of trees, flowers, and lower plants is produced by ideal moisture and a temperate climate.

Forest Openings: The Balds

Most mountains show mosaic patterns of vegetation noticeable at a distance, or on scenic postcards. In the Smokies high country this zoning is conspicuous. These mountains rival the Rockies for all such contrasts, except for naked rock above timberline.

There is no climatic treeline—roughly an elevation above which trees cannot survive—in the Smokies. But two important treeless communities, called "balds" by the early settlers, give this above-timber effect here.

The baldness is not that of bare rock, but rather a mountain-top interruption to the forest cover. The two types, grass balds and heath balds, are alike only in appearance from a distance, and in their preference for mountain summits.

The Cherokees wove the balds into their religion and folklore. Mountaineers grazed stock on the grass balds and cursed the heath balds as "slicks" or "hells." Botanists began to publish explanations for these balds a century ago but you can still formulate your own theory because there are no agreed-upon answers. The more careful the

study, the more puzzles arise. But the key in both cases seems to be *disturbance,* the successive destruction of generations of tree seedlings.

For heath balds the most obvious tree-killing agent is fire and so fire was advanced as an explanation for their origin. Shrubs can burn to the ground and grow back quickly, sprouting from their roots. Mountain laurel, rhododendron, blueberry, huckleberry, and sand myrtle all do this. It was theorized that where fire knocks out the tree layer, there are the heath balds. But the rub is that some balds show no signs of fire and yet are not nursing young trees.

Landslides eliminate trees, and winter winds may also discourage tree growth. Heath balds persevere where slopes are steep, soil is peaty and acidic, and the elevation tops 1,200 meters (4,000 feet).

Today the grass balds are a mosaic of shrubs, grasses, and young trees. Open patches may be clearly dominated by grasses but the total number of plant species present on grass balds is greater than the number present on heath balds.

Explanations of the origin of grass balds have been much debated but no theory has been accepted for them all. We do know that most grass balds were used as high elevation pastures in the 1800s and early 1900s, and when the park was established the grass balds were much more open than today. Most Southern Appalachian grass balds are being quickly invaded by trees and shrubs. The National Park Service is developing plans to keep two Smokies balds open. Despite their appearance, grassy balds have no floristic relation to true alpine or arctic tundra vegetation.

The sundew, a bog plant common in the far North, persists on one grass bald, near a spring. What look like dew droplets are actually gluey traps for insects, which this carnivorous plant kills and absorbs.

Flame azalea thrives on grassy balds. At Gregory Bald it hybridizes with other azaleas, producing an array of colored flowers that botanists call a "hybrid swarm."

When settlers grazed stock on the grass balds, many common weeds such as dandelions were introduced. Before settlement deer and elk probably grazed here, and may have helped keep out encroaching trees.

The Trout's World

The rays of the early morning sun bombard the tops of the trees spread above the headwaters of Forney Creek. Some penetrate the canopy to make light patches in the lower layers of the forest. But few break through the rhododendron thickets along the stream to illuminate its mossy rocks, its foam, and its clear pools. Down in the darkness beneath overhanging shrubs, hanging in the current near the bottom of a pool, a brook trout waits for the stream to bring it food. With dark mottling along its back, red spots on its olive sides, and pale orange edging on its lower fins, the fish is beautiful. It is also small, about 18 centimeters (7 inches) long, and lean, for it lives in a harsh environment where food is scarce, the water is cold and acidic, and floods and thick ice can scour. This is one of only a few trout in the pool because there is not enough food for many.

The trout fed little during the night and now its hunger is acute. Carefully it watches the rippling surface for insects, spiders, crayfish, salamanders, and worms, or any animal life caught and carried down by the current. But nothing appears. It noses up to a rock where earlier in the summer it had found caddisfly larvae fastened in their tubular little cases made of tiny pebbles. Now none are left on the surface of the rock accessible to the trout. It searches other rocks and eventually finds one caddisfly larva and a small mayfly nymph, flattened against the under side. The trout dashes at a small salamander, which escapes under another rock. Three crayfish also inhabit the pool but they are too big for this particular trout to eat.

The presence of trout somehow symbolizes wild nature and pristine beauty. Pools such as this one at the foot of Grotto Falls on Roaring Fork, are quiet forest gems that cause the finger of many an angler to twitch uncontrollably.

The trout's hunger increases and still nothing edible washes over the miniature waterfall at the head of the pool. But suddenly sand and gravel begin dropping in and there is a pulsing in the flow of water. Upstream a bear has crossed and in its crossing it has knocked a beetle off an overhanging branch. The beetle floats down one little cataract after another, its legs kicking wildly and its wet wings vainly buzzing. There is a splash as the trout strikes. The beetle will sustain it through one more day.

In contrast to the brook trout's life in the headwaters, the rainbow trout would appear to have an easier time in the lower reaches of park streams. Here the pools are larger, the stream gradient is less, the water is less acidic, and nutrients are more abundant. These conditions allow more plant and animal life to exist, and therefore create more food for trout. Also, at these lower elevations, where the water is deeper, winter ice cannot form so solidly as higher up. These waters are not exactly teeming with aquatic life, but they are adequate for rainbow trout.

Trout do not generally remain active continuously. They tend to feed in the late afternoon, at night, and early in the morning, resting at the bottom of a pool during midday. Both brook and rainbow trout will have resting sites, day and night, and feeding sites.

A favored feeding site is often the head of the pool, where a trout will have the first chance to seize insects or other organisms carried into the pool. It also has the option of hunting many of the forms of life that live in the stream with it: insect larvae and nymphs of many kinds, aquatic beetles and spiders, crayfish, leeches and worms, water-mites, snails, salamanders, tadpoles, and the smaller fish.

Among the more common fishes that live in rainbow trout territory in low elevation, low gradient streams are sculpins, dace, hogsuckers, river chubs, shiners, and stonerollers. Hogsuckers, which reach 30 centimeters (a foot) or more in length, can be seen in many large, quiet pools. There they search for food on the bottom with their downward protruding lips. Dace and shiners, members of the minnow family, are very small fish and some species are brilliantly colored. The river chub and stoneroller, also minnows, are larger; the stoneroller occasionally reaches 28 centimeters (11 inches). Locally known as "hornyhead" and enjoyed as a food fish, the abundant stoneroller may limit the numbers of rainbow trout in some stretches of stream because of its own spawning activities. Rainbows lay their eggs on gravelly areas in early spring. A month or so later, before the trout eggs have hatched, stonerollers frequently build their nests in the same places, covering or scattering the trout eggs in the process. This sort of competition was probably not expected or considered when rainbows were introduced to the Smokies; nevertheless, the trout do manage to perpetuate themselves.

No doubt the most peculiar creature in the lower sections of park streams is the hellbender, a huge, grayish salamander with a loose fold of skin along each side.

Commonly reaching 30 centimeters (a foot) and occasionally more than 60 centimeters (2 feet) in length, hellbenders hide under rocks and debris in swift water and feed on fish and other animals up to the size of crayfish. Below elevations of about 500 meters (1,600 feet) smallmouth bass, rock bass, and brightly colored little darters appear in park waters. Brown trout, an introduced species that has apparently entered the park from farther downstream, live in the lower sections of some streams, and may be found in the headwaters of some streams. Of the three species of trout in the Smokies, browns generally prove most difficult to catch.

Since early in this century when rainbow trout were introduced, and possibly even before, brook trout have been retreating upstream in these mountains. In the late 19th century, brook trout occurred as low as 500 meters (1,600 feet); now they are found mostly above 915 meters (3,000 feet). The effects of logging and competition from rainbows are the most frequently suggested reasons for this retreat. Logging, which began on a large scale in the Smokies about 1900, brought with it many fires. The resulting exposure to full sunlight caused the warming of low-elevation sections of streams. Erosion of the denuded land added heavy loads of sediment to the streams. These changed conditions, and possibly heavy fishing pressure, apparently speeded the disappearance of brook trout from the lower elevations. Rainbows were introduced and proved able to survive. In the '20s and '30s it was noted that rainbows occurred in streams up to about the upper limit of logging, and that brook trout occupied streams above that point. Now, however, streams are once again shaded by forests their full length; but brook trout, instead of moving back down, seem to have retreated higher upstream. It appears that the larger, more aggressive rainbows somehow prevent brook trout from re-occupying their lost waters.

The National Park Service is concerned for the future of the Smokies' one species of native trout, and especially for the few isolated populations of brookies that may still remain unmixed with populations of brook trout introduced from other parts of the country. On some streams, waterfalls provide effective barriers to the advance of rainbow trout, and use of artificial barriers for this purpose has been considered. Stringent fishing regulations may help the easily caught brook trout—and the gluttonous poaching that sometimes eliminates large numbers of brook trout from long stretches of a stream must be stopped. This type of management problem, how to preserve native species and reduce the impact of exotic ones, is common in national parks. It is only one aspect of a larger problem: How do we maintain natural ecosystems in parks? This basic aspect of the national park idea is difficult to implement in a country where human influence is so ubiquitous.

Quite a few animals of the Smokies depend on streams and their organisms without living entirely in them. They live with one foot in the water and one foot on land, as it were. Raccoons out hunting at night patrol streams, alert for frogs, crayfish, and mussels. Mink pursue fish, crayfish, and other animals underwater, flowing downstream through the foam as effortlessly as water itself. Kingfishers perch on overhanging branches to plunge headfirst after small fish. Their loud, rattling calls can be heard on the lower courses of many streams. The small Louisiana waterthrush, a warbler, teeters on rocks in the torrent, searching for aquatic insects. It nests on stream banks or behind waterfalls. Its song, a lovely descending jumble of notes, cascades like the water of its haunts. Harmless water snakes, mottled brown somewhat like the water moccasin (which does not occur in the Smokies), like to sun on limbs or debris near the water. Frogs, fish, salamanders, and crayfish form most of their diet. Of the park's few species of frogs, the green frog is the one most likely to be found in streams. Aquatic turtles are even less common; most numerous is the snapping turtle, a wanderer that sometimes reaches the middle elevations in the park.

Ducks, herons, and other large aquatic birds, scarce in the park because there are no large bodies of water, do appear occasionally. On the section of Abrams Creek that flows through Cades Cove you may surprise a wood duck or green heron. Though not very productive of plant food, Fontana Lake on the south border of the park sometimes serves as a resting place for migrating waterfowl.

Perhaps we humans could be considered semi-aquatic ourselves, so strongly does water attract us. In the Smokies people love to visit waterfalls, plunge into favorite swimming holes, play among the rocks and white water, and fish up and down the streams. One of my favorite activities is simple stream-watching. Just pick a sunny rock, sit down with your lunch, and watch. That's all there is to it. Trout will eventually grow bold enough to come out of hiding. Birds fly out of the dense forest to feed in the sunlit shrubs along the stream. Butterflies wander down this open avenue, and dragonflies dart after winged prey. Sometimes the unusual happens. One fine October day as I was just finishing my sandwich, a little red squirrel appeared on the opposite shore, edged down a rock to the water, and plunged in. It drifted with the current and then scrambled out on a rock near me. A swimming squirrel I had never expected to see.

In the Smokies you are seldom far from the sound of water. These tumbling streams—the Little Pigeon, the Oconaluftee, Roaring Fork, Hazel Creek, and all their many brothers—have voices as various as a hound dog's. They talk, murmur, shout, and sing, rising and falling in tone. Porters Creek once actually convinced me that people were talking and playing guitars on its bank. This is the soul music of the mountains.

Smokies Trout

Brook trout, or "spec," are a glimpse of nature at her best. Their colorful delicacy is a sharp contrast to the mountains' mass. The three-toned fins most easily distinguish it from other species while it swims. A mountaineer here once paid the local dentist 200 trout—caught in a morning—for some dental work, as attested by account books. Park regulations now prohibit catching the brook trout because it has lost so much of its original territory that its numbers have been severely reduced.

Brown trout, a European fish, has entered the park recently. It inhabits the park's lower waters, which provide the warmer, slower conditions it prefers. It will eat its own young as well as those of competing rainbow and brook trout.

Rainbow trout were introduced from the West during the logging era via milk cans to improve fishing. They are larger and more aggressive than brookies.

The streams and rivers of the Smokies are famous for their purity. All who come to these mountains are impressed by the beauty of the waterways that have carved their way into the lush wilderness. More than 300 streams flow throughout the park. To many of us these streams mean only one thing, trout. Actually, more than 70 species of fish have been collected in the park, such as chubs, shiners, minnows, dace, catfish, suckers, sculpins, darters, and even lamprey.

Trout live in fast-flowing water where their streamlined bodies enable them to maintain themselves in the current, often close to the stream bottom. Brookies, especially, require such pure water that they are often considered a clean water "index."

This little creature is known as a mayfly, one of the five insects most widely imitated by artificial fly patterns. The imitations seek to simulate, as dry, wet, or nymph patterns, the insects' larval and adult stages and their aquatic habits.

45

Male Adams

Adams Variant

Yellow Forney Creek

Dark Cahill

Royal Wulff

Humpy or Guffus Bug

Olive Caddis

Light Cahill

Grey Hackle Peacock

Leadwing Coachman

Secret Weapon

Yellow Wooly Worm

Yellow Hammer (antique gold)

Yellow Hammer (peacock)

Light Cahill Nymph

To rile up trout anglers just assert that one fly pattern is the best. But in fly fishing areas such as the Smokies, a few patterns inevitably emerge as favorites. Here as elsewhere, most artificial flies imitate five varieties of insects common to most waters: mayflies, caddisflies, stoneflies, alderflies, and ants. There are, in all, about 5,000 sorts of human-tied flies in existence. Does that sound overwhelming? Well, there are probably hundreds of thousands of varieties of insects which trout may feed upon at one time or another. The following advice will help you narrow your choice.

Dry Flies *Mayfly imitations:* Light Cahill, Quill Gordon, Royal Coachman, Dark Hendrickson. *Caddis imitations:* Henryville Special. *Ant imitations:* Black Ant, Red Ant.

Wet Fly and Nymphs Black Woolly Worm, Hendrickson, Light Cahill, Hare's Ear, March Brown.

Streamers Olive Mateuka, Muddler Minnow (imitates grasshopper or sculpin).

Watch out for low-hanging branches!

Female Adams

❶ Head
❷ Wing
❸ Body
❹ Tail
❺ Hackle

Choosing a pattern may challenge today's trout angler in the Smokies, but choosing your bait does not. Fishing is confined to artificial lures only. No bait is allowed. Pictured here is Mrs. Clem Enloe. She was 84 years old and lived on Tight Run Branch when Joseph S. Hall took this photo. She was the last person—and the only one in her own day, in fact—allowed to use worms as bait in the park. She was also allowed to fish here any season of the year because she flat refused to obey the new park's newly-instituted fishing regulations. Park rangers didn't have the heart to throw the book at her. "I was told that if I took her a box of snuff, she would let me take her picture," photographer Hall said. That's the snuff in her blouse. Someone later suggested that the rangers should have tried snuff too.

We ask that you, however, please follow all fishing regulations!

Logging

"These are the heaviest and most beautiful hard-wood forests of the continent," read a 1901 report from President Theodore Roosevelt to Congress. Lumber entrepreneurs were impressed, and the Little River watershed was sold that year for about $9.70 per hectare ($4.00 per acre)—all 34,400 hectares (85,000 acres) of it! Throughout the Smokies, entire watersheds were staked off like mining claims. Largest of all was a timbered plot owned by the Champion Coated Paper Company. It included Deep Creek, Greenbrier Cove, and the headwaters of the Oconaluftee River.

Logging came to the Smokies on a large scale about 1900. Settlers had always cut trees here, but the lumber companies and their money and methods injected a major new element. Instead of a few oxen dragging heavy logs to mill, the lumber companies introduced railroads, steam loaders, and steam skidders on the landscape. As you drive from Elkmont toward Townsend along the park road, you are driving atop the old railbed that was laid down by the Little River Logging Company.

was the most valuable wood, and most scarce. Tall, straight yellow-poplar turned out to be the most profitable because of its large volume.

New towns sprang up: Elkmont, Crestmont, Proctor, Ravensford, and Smokemont. These provided something new to the Smokies, a cash market. For a time, one egg would "buy" a child a week's supply of candy. Local families sold farm products to the loggers and sawmill men.

The Smokies yielded board feet of lumber by the millions. Cherry

The devastation seen in the photograph on the facing page is the aftermath of a fire that was set by sparks belched out of logging equipment, an unfortunate source of several devastating fires in logging's heyday.

The ravages of logging led to fires, and the fires led to flooding. Many fires were set by the flaming sparks from locomotives or log skidders. More than 20 disastrous fires took place in the 1920s alone. A two-month series of fires burned over parts of Clingmans Dome, Silers Bald, and Mt. Guyot. Intense destruction oc-

curred in the Charlie's Bunion area of The Sawteeth in 1925. Hikers on the Appalachian Trail still see the effects of this fire.

The fires created conditions for massive flooding. Parched soils were no longer secured by living roots and the dense mat of plants that makes the Smokies world famous today. Streams and rivers flooded, carrying unusually heavy loads of sediment. These conditions were intolerable for the native Southern Appalachian brook trout and apparently speeded their disappearance from lower elevations.

Rainbow trout were introduced and proved able to survive. More recently brown trout were successfully introduced. The brookies now occupy less than half the territory they did in the 1930s.

Some flooding is still common today. This is natural. The Smokies get their fair share of rainfall, making seasonal flooding expected. And every few years prolonged or bad storms can cause unusually heavy flooding of the streams and rivers. Here you see the Little Pigeon River in flood near park headquarters in 1979. Whenever Smokies streams or rivers are flooded it is very dangerous to attempt crossing them. Don't try it. Revise your itinerary instead.

What about fires today? Lightning-caused fire is as ancient as the mountains themselves and has always been a part of the forest's life process. Some tree species actually depend on fire for regeneration, such as the pin cherry. And the heath bald shrubs, such as blueberry and mountain-laurel, prosper after a light burn. Fire is necessary as well to dozens of flowering plants which quickly seed new forest openings the fire creates.

We have long viewed fire on wildlands as a catastrophe, and indeed it is often a piteous sight.

But the urge to suppress fire completely sometimes results in other unsatisfactory conditions. On many large public land areas limited wildfires are now allowed to burn if they don't threaten private property or human lives.

The Evolution of Abundance

Diversity is the biological keynote of the Great Smoky Mountains. Within the national park have been found about 1,500 species of flowering plants, among which are some 100 trees. There are around 2,000 fungi, 50 mammals, 200 birds, and 70 fishes, or more than in the fresh waters of any other national park on our continent. There are about 80 reptiles and amphibians, among which are 22 salamanders, which is probably as many as can be found in any similar-sized area in North America. Present conditions, such as warmth, abundant moisture, and a diversity of environments brought about by the height and dissection of the mountains, are partly responsible for this biotic wealth. But time, the many millions of years this land has been above the sea and south of the ice, has also been an important factor. It has been a span long enough for a great many species of plants and animals to get here and find a niche and for other species to evolve in the region. The story of the arrival and evolution of the present flora and fauna is intimately linked with the dramatic history of our continent.

We can only guess what life existed here during the 130 million years of the Mesozoic era, because no rocks from this period exist in the Smokies. But we can imagine that dinosaurs and primitive birds and mammals roamed the region, as they did other parts of the continent. Toward the close of the Mesozoic, flowering plants evolved and rapidly became the dominant type of vegetation. We can guess that some of these first magnolias, elms, and oaks grew right here in the ancestral Smokies. Newly evolved bees probably helped to pollinate some of the flowering plants.

The story becomes clearer and the life forms become more and more familiar to us during the 65 million years of the Cenozoic, the present era. In the first half of the Cenozoic, subtropical vegetation grew in the southern United States and temperate vegetation grew north to the Arctic. As these plants would indicate by their ability to grow here, this was a time of warm or mild climates throughout the Northern Hemisphere. Land bridges between North America and Eurasia, by way of the Bering Strait and perhaps Greenland, allowed the spread of a remarkably homogeneous flora throughout the then-

The Smokies is an ancient landmass. Its plantlife may have evolved uninterruptedly for more than 200 million years. Continental Ice Age glaciation did not reach this far south, and as the Atlantic Ocean has repeatedly inundated most of North America, the Smokies remained an island.

temperate parts of these two continents. The Great Smokies, with their feet in the South and, as it were, their head climatically in the North, must have had both subtropical and temperate vegetation early in the Cenozoic era.

During the second half of the Cenozoic, a cooling trend set in. The widespread "Arctotertiary" vegetation of the northern latitudes moved southwards through North America and Eurasia. By the end of the Tertiary, which includes all but the past two to three million years of the Cenozoic, the vegetation zones of North America were probably very similar to those of the present. In the Smokies the trees probably ranged from southern types, such as sweetgum, at low elevations through the great mixture of cove forests and possibly to spruce and fir at the highest elevations. After a long period of gradual change in climate, the stage was set for the drastic events of the Pleistocene.

It is hard for us to imagine what an ice age must have been like in our country. Perhaps the only way to imagine it is to visit the Antarctic or one of the great glaciers in Alaska, and to watch giant slabs of ice fall from those towering walls. Then . . . mentally transport the scene to the Hudson River valley or to the flatlands of Illinois, while magnifying the thickness of those glaciers several times over. Then imagine the surface of that great ice sheet stretching all the way to northern Canada.

If you had stood near the front of that massive ice sheet, you would have felt the cold air flowing off it. How far south that cold, dense air flowed and to what extent it affected temperatures in the southern states are unanswered questions. But undoubtedly temperatures were lowered throughout North America and perhaps farther south. Some scientists postulate a drop of 5.5 degrees Celsius (10 degrees Fahrenheit) in mean annual temperatures in southern United States. The high pressure that developed over the ice sheet would have pushed storm tracks southward, increasing precipitation in the South.

Such continental ice sheets advanced at least four times as climates cooled, and as many times they retreated during warmer intervals. With each advance and the consequent cooler, wetter climate, there was undoubtedly a southward shift of vegetation belts. In the mountains there would also have been a downward shift of forest types, particularly those of the higher elevations. That is, the higher elevation species would begin to grow down the slope. In sheltered coves temperatures probably did not drop as much as they did higher up or out in the open lowlands, and soils in coves were deeper and more fertile. The coves of the Southern Appalachians thus may have formed a refuge for many temperate species of plants, including some forced southward by the spreading ice. This is a factor in today's biotic richness or abundance in the Smokies.

On top of the Smokies and other high mountains of the Southern Appalachians, tundra (treeless areas) may have developed as winter climates became too cold and windy even for spruce and fir, which is the situation today on high peaks of the Adirondacks and White Mountains in New England. Accumulations of blocky boulders in higher parts of the Smokies resemble block fields in the northern Appalachians that probably were formed above timberline in late stages of glaciation. From the location of block fields, geologists postulate a treeline in the Smokies somewhere between 900 and 1,500 meters (3,000 and 5,000 feet) elevation during the last glacial period, some 15,000 to 25,000 years ago. If islands of tundra did exist in the Southern Appalachians, it is not likely that tundra mammals would have migrated from the tundra bordering the ice front through the intervening forest to reach such Arctic pastures in the sky. But some birds might have. Water pipits, which today nest in the Arctic and above timberline on our Western mountains, might have bred on these patches of southern tundra. And the few snow buntings which have been seen wintering on Southern Appalachian balds may have been returning to ancestral nesting grounds of the species.

Although Pleistocene tundra in the Smokies is a rather speculative notion, it seems certain that spruce-fir forest existed below today's 1,400-meter (4,600-foot) limit. This supposition is supported by the fact that fossil pollen and other fragments of spruce and fir have been found in several lowland bog deposits of the South.

During the last Ice Age the Southern Appalachian spruce-fir forests and their animals must have been a richer version of the plant-animal community that exists in this zone today, for at the peak of the ice advance northern plants and animals probably could migrate along a continuous avenue of this boreal forest in the Appalachians. Bones from cave deposits at Natural Chimneys in Virginia's Shenandoah Valley indicate that such northern animals as porcupines, snowshoe hares, pine martens, fishers, spruce grouse, and gray jays, as well as the now extinct longnosed peccary and giant beaver, roamed that area 10,000 to 15,000 years ago. The still existing species mentioned above now live farther north in the forests of New England and Canada. If such animals could live during the late Pleistocene at 450 meters (1,500 feet) in Virginia, many and perhaps all of them might well have lived at higher elevations in the Smokies. In the case of porcupines, archeological records from nearby regions in fact support this idea.

After the retreat of the last ice sheet a warm, dry period set in and caused the development of grasslands as far east as Ohio. To what extent this change in climate may have affected the Smokies is not known. But it may have been responsible for the development of the beech gaps: as the spruce-fir forests were forced ever higher, beeches and yellow birches followed in their wake. The once continuous band of spruce-fir forest through the Southern Appalachians would then have been broken into patches as it migrated to higher elevations—and disappeared entirely on the lower mountains. Today such forest is restricted in the Southern Appalachians to the highest parts of eastern West Virginia, southwestern Virginia, western North Carolina, and areas in and just north of the Great Smokies. During the warmer, drier period following glaciation, boreal forest must have been even smaller in extent.

Another consequence of warming was the northward migration of plants and animals into territory vacated by the ice sheet (north of the Ohio River and Long Island). The result today in northeastern United States is a broad patchwork of forest types, each type dominated by a few species, as in beech-maple or beech-birch-white pine forests. This stands in contrast to the diversity of the cove forests from which the migrants extended. Cove forests still harbor individuals of all these species.

What happens next? Has the Pleistocene epoch really ended or are we merely between glaciers, awaiting the next invasion of ice? For the Smokies the question implies others: Will the forest zones move up or down the mountainsides? How will this affect animal life?

While terrestrial life in the mountains flourished during the continent's climatic swings, aquatic life fared equally well. Within Great Smoky Mountains National Park live some 70 species of fish. Contrast this with the number in Shenandoah National Park in the Blue Ridge of Virginia, which has only about 25 species. Why so many in the Smokies? The answer parallels the situation for plants and terrestrial animals: diversity of environments and plenty of time. All the streams of the Smokies lie within the Tennessee River drainage, which is part of the Mississippi River drainage. The Tennessee River has more species of fish than any other river in North America, because of its many environments (lowland, plateau, and mountain); the vastness of the Mississippi drainage; its existence for many millions of years; and its Pleistocene history. During glacial periods many species of fish were forced southward by ice and cold glacial water. The Tennessee River system offered them a refuge just as Southern Appalachian coves offered a refuge for plants. Even the Mississippi itself was a less favorable haven because it received most of the meltwater. In the headwaters of the Tennessee, the streams of the Smokies thus benefit from their contact with an ancient, relatively undisturbed river system. Within the park, stream environments range from cold and fast to comparatively cool and slow, with large, deep pools.

While most of the present plant and animal species of the Smokies have ranges that extend far beyond these mountains, and while many of these have spread here from other areas of origin, a few are restricted solely to the Smokies. This suggests that they may have evolved here. One such plant is Rugel's groundsel, a member of the Composite family that grows to about 28 centimeters (11 inches) high and bears large, cylindrical clusters of tiny golden flowers. This plant, abundant in the park's spruce-fir forests, has not been found outside the Smokies. This suggests that it evolved in the Southern Appalachians and that after the last glacial period, when connection with other sections of spruce-fir forest was broken, it persisted or survived only in the Smokies. By comparison, the Fraser fir, though most abundant in the Smokies, also occurs north to southwestern Virginia on the highest mountains, indicating that it evolved at some earlier, colder time when spruce-fir forest was more nearly continuous. The red-cheeked salamander, a striking creature, is probably the sole vertebrate found exclusively in the Smokies. Many other species of salamanders, however, are restricted to parts of the southern end of the Appalachians and probably evolved there, where the cool, wet climate and diverse topography provide ideal conditions for this group of animals. How many other species of plants and animals evolved in the region and subsequently spread far beyond this point of origin we can only conjecture.

Natural History Sampler

These eight pages sample the abundant life of the Smokies, from flowering plants and shrubs to birds, mammals, reptiles, and amphibians.

Species are shown for various reasons. You may want to identify the common species you see in the wild. Other species are uncommon and you are not likely to see them. Still others are uncommonly beautiful, and we don't want you to miss seeing at least their pictures.

Information, drawings, and photographs of bears and wild boars are found in the "Bears, Boars and Acorns" chapter.

Jack-in-the-pulpit

Scarlet painted-cup

Painted trillium

Coreopsis

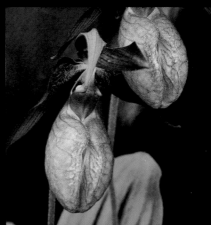

Pink lady's-slipper

Turk's-cap lily

Orange hawkweed

Bird's-foot violet

Passion-flower

Fringe-tree

Dog-hobble

Flame azalea

Redbud

Mountain silverbell

Witch-hobble

60

Umbrella magnolia

Flowering dogwood

Catawba rhododendron

Fire cherry

Yellow-poplar

Mountain laurel

Barred owl

Cardinal

Wild turkey

Yellow warbler

Common flicker

Tufted titmouse

Spotted skunk

Whitetail deer

Cottontail rabbit

Bobcat

Deermouse

Opossum

Fence lizard

Ringneck snake

Leopard frog

Gray treefrog

Timber rattlesnake

Copperhead

Pine snake

American toad

Bears, Boars and Acorns

As frosts touch the earth and the reds and yellows of fall creep down the mountainsides, oaks, hickories, beeches, and other trees shed their fruits. Many animals will join in the harvest of this fruit, but several, especially bear, deer, wild boar, gray squirrel, chipmunk, turkey, and ruffed grouse, are particularly dependent on this mast, as it is called, for their autumn and winter welfare. With the chestnut gone these animals must rely mostly on acorns. Oaks, unlike the chestnut, do not produce consistently, but fruit abundantly some years and fail in others. In the poor years, when competition for mast is keen, the effects are starvation, wandering, and mass migrations. The appearance and multiplication of European wild boars in the park have only added to the pressure on the native animal species. Acorn shortages bring into sharp focus the life styles and survival systems of the mast-dependent animals. From among these the wild boar emerges as an ecological villain, although we should perhaps cast man, who introduced the boar here, in that role.

The loss of the chestnut illustrates how a change in one element can irrevocably alter an entire ecosystem. As the chestnuts of the Smokies died, their place was taken primarily by chestnut oak, northern red oak, red maple, hemlock, and silverbell. The annual mast crop suffered from this change in two ways. First, only about half of the replacement trees were mast-bearing oaks. Second, oaks are not dependable mast-bearers. Mast failures seem to result mainly from spring freezes during the pollinating and fertilization of oak flowers. Chestnuts bloomed in the first two weeks of June when the danger of frost was slight and so they bore well nearly every year. This difference in flowering time has had reverberations throughout the animal world within these mountains. By looking into the life histories and population dynamics of some of the acorn eaters we may get some idea of the nature and extent of those reverberations.

Whitetail deer prefer young forests and mixtures of forest and field because in these areas an abundance of shrubs and herbaceous plants provides ample food. The mature forests of the Smokies have relatively little forage near the ground and so they support only small numbers

Oak trees add the brilliance of their turning leaves to fall's burst of colors. The oaks' acorn crop is also important winter food for several forest creatures. Chestnuts once supplied winter food, too, but a blight virtually eliminated the chestnut trees earlier this century, adding to the importance of acorns.

of deer. In the Cades Cove area, however, the lush meadows and second-growth forest feed several hundred deer. In the fall deer join in the mast harvest, but they do not depend on it as do the bears, gray squirrels, wild boars, and chipmunks. Deer have the option of eating twigs, buds, and herbaceous plants. They eat acorns, however, and this nutritious food will help them enter winter in good condition. Deer mating takes place from September to November in the Smokies, as the mature males each run with a female for several days, then hunt for another. In winter the bucks shed their antlers and join the does and yearlings. In May or June the does give birth to their spotted fawns, usually twins. The summer bands you see in Cades Cove are again separated by sex as the bucks once again grow antlers in preparation for the autumn battles.

Now that wolves and other large predators are gone from the Smokies, starvation and disease are the principal checks on deer numbers. Late in 1971 a disease that causes massive bleeding struck the herd in Cades Cove, killing many of the deer and a few cattle. But by the following spring an increase in the production of offspring and the influx of deer from nearby areas brought the herd back almost to its former number.

Gray squirrel numbers fluctuate even more dramatically, as populations build up and then collapse, but these oscillations occur even when food is adequate. Until recently, some observers thought these oscillations were amplified by mast failures, but apparently they are not. In the Smokies, gray squirrels are found mostly in the oak and beech forest of the lower and middle elevations, while their smaller cousins, the red squirrels, stick more to the upper elevations. In years of extreme low population swings such as 1946 and 1968, many migrating squirrels have been killed on the highways; others have even been seen attempting to swim Fontana Lake. The loss of gray squirrels in 1946 was estimated at 90 percent for some watersheds.

Turkeys and ruffed grouse both feed heavily on acorns in the fall, although they, like the deer, have other possibilities. Turkey and grouse also feed on the fruits of dogwood and wild grape; beechnuts in good years; seeds; and buds. A statewide study in Virginia found that acorns supplied about one-quarter of the annual diet of wild turkeys, and this proportion is much higher in fall. Acorns are also a top food item in fall for ruffed grouse.

We come now to the two chief antagonists in the

annual mast hunt, bears and wild boars. The arrival of wild boars in the park has meant added competition for bears, as well as many other disruptive ecological effects. By considering the population dynamics and seasonal activities of these two species, we get a clear contrast between their roles. One fits in with the forest "establishment" and one clearly does not.

How many bears live in the park? This is difficult to determine because bears are secretive and tend to wander. The National Park Service estimates that numbers usually range from about 400 up to about 600, depending on reproduction, food availability, extent of poaching, and other factors. The estimates are based on intensive research by the University of Tennessee in the northwest quarter of the park.

From about December to March black bears sleep, although they occasionally come out for brief periods. During the University of Tennessee studies it was learned, to the surprise of many, that bears in the Great Smokies had a preference for denning in hollow trees, sometimes as much as 15 meters (50 feet) above the ground. Typically, such a tree has been broken off by storms and provides an entrance and some sort of platform within that supports the bear. In such a den, or one in a protected place on the ground, the female in alternate years gives birth to tiny cubs weighing about a half-kilo (18 ounces) apiece.

Most bears leave their dens in late March or April and from then until early summer, when berries begin ripening, they find food scarce. Black bears are primarily vegetarians, though they eat almost any animal matter they can find, from ants to large mammals, as well as carrion. In spring they graze grasses heavily. Squawroot, a fleshy, conelike, parasitic plant, is a favored food then, so much so that local people call squawroot bear potato or bear cabbage. Roots and insect grubs also help to see the bears through spring, a time so lean for them that droppings are seldom seen on the trails. At this season bears roam widely at all elevations. Mating occurs in early summer.

From late July until early September the bears concentrate on berries, especially the blackberries growing in open places such as ridgetops and balds, and the blueberries most abundant in open oak-pine woods. Since insects and vertebrate animals are most numerous in summer, bears harvest them more frequently then than at other times. They especially seek beetles and nests of yellowjackets. With throngs of campers in the park bears investigate this source of food, too. National Park Service management practices are aimed at ending such scavenging—which makes bears both dependent on and dangerous to people—and ensuring that the animals live out their normal lives in the forest. Being deprived of garbage will work no hardship because, for bears and most other animals, summer is the season of abundance.

As fall progresses blackberries, blueberries, and beetles diminish in the diet and acorns and beechnuts increase until they become the primary sustenance. Bears are particularly fond of white oak acorns, the sweetest. In their eagerness the huge animals, which sometimes reach 200 kilos (450 pounds) in weight, even climb trees and crawl out on the branches as far as they can to eat the fruits or break off and drop the branch tips for consumption on the ground. They also relish black cherries and serviceberries. A park naturalist told me of watching a very large bear climb a 5-centimeter (2-inch) thick serviceberry on Spence Field, bending the tree double. Throughout the Southern Appalachians you can see small serviceberries broken down like this by bears in their quest for the fruits.

In most years the mast crop is adequate for all the animals dependent on it, but in the years of failure bears are hard pressed to find enough to eat. They wander down out of the mountains in search of food. In such years many are killed by hunters outside the national park. The loss of bears in some of the poorest mast years may be one-third to one-half of the park's bear population.

Enter now the European wild boar. Its history in the Smokies is another classic example, along with the chestnut blight fungus, balsam woolly aphid, Norway rat, starling, and a host of other pests, of the damage that can be done by introducing an organism to territory outside its normal range. The wild boars in the Smokies are believed to be descendants of animals, purportedly of stock from Germany, that escaped from a game preserve on Hooper Bald, southwest of Fontana Lake, in the early 1920s. They were first detected in the park about 1950. By the early 1960s wild boars, now with some admixture of domestic pig blood, had spread east to Newfound Gap and, in the lower country, to Cosby and possibly Cataloochee. Their occupation of the entire park seemed imminent.

So now the Smokies have a wild counterpart of the

domestic hog, the staple livestock animal that mountaineers once ran year-round in these woods. Horace
Kephart's vivid description of the hog in the 1920s applies
almost as well to today's European wild boar: "In physique
and mentality, the razorback differs even more from a
domestic hog than a wild goose does from a tame one,"
Kephart wrote. "Shaped in front like a thin wedge, he
can go through laurel thickets like a bear. Armored with
tough hide cushioned by bristles, he despises thorns,
brambles, and rattlesnakes, alike. His extravagantly long
snout can scent like a cat's, and yet burrow, uproot,
overturn, as if made of metal."

The hog's long legs, thin flanks, and pliant hoofs fitted
it to run like a deer and climb like a goat, Kephart
claimed, calling it "a warrior born" who was also a first
rate strategist.

The European wild boar sometimes attains a height of
nearly a meter (three feet) at the shoulder and a weight of
100 kilos (220 pounds). It is built rather like a bison, the
hindquarters sloping down from the shoulders. The long,
hairy-tipped tail and, in the male, well-developed tusks
also distinguish it from its domestic counterpart. Obvi-
ously, this is a formidable animal, as numerous boar
hunters who have been treed by it or watched it cut up
their dogs can attest. Normally, however, wild boars are
not dangerous and run at the sight or scent of man. One
evening, standing in a yard where a boar had rooted the
night before, I asked a long-time boar observer about the
animal's pugnacity.

"They won't attack you unless they're wounded or
hemmed," this observer related. "I've tried to get them to
charge me. Even picked up a squealing piglet once, but
the sow didn't attack."

Wild boars feed mostly at night. Campers near balds
in the western section of the park sometimes see them
or hear their grunts and snorts as they run away. The
females and young travel about in family groups but the
males are loners. Though the animals are elusive, spend-
ing their days resting in dense cover, the signs of their
rooting are very obvious on balds, in beech gaps and
open fields, and along trails in moist woods.

Wild boars move seasonally in quest of food. In spring
they eat a lot of grass, as well as succulent roots and the
upper parts of wildflowers, which are especially abundant in cove forests and high-elevation beech forests. In
summer they continue eating grass and other herbaceous plants but also seek huckleberries, blueberries,

and blackberries. When acorns, hickory nuts, beech-nuts, and other tree fruits start falling, they turn their attention to these, which in abundant years can carry the boars through winter. When the mast fails they feed heavily on tubers of wild yam and the outer layer of pitch pine roots. Throughout the year they supplement this vegetable diet with whatever invertebrates, salamanders, snakes, rodents, and other small animals they can root out or catch. Carrion and garbage are always welcome, too. The wild boar, as classic an omnivore as his domestic cousin, will eat almost anything.

Aside from the competition they give other masteaters in the critical fall season, wild boars upset the ecological balance in additional ways. Susan Bratton, research biologist with the National Park Service's Uplands Field Research Laboratory here in the Smokies, has made detailed studies of boar damage. She found that in some areas boars had greatly reduced the numbers of certain wildflowers, such as spring-beauty, yellow adder's-tongue, and wake-robin. Many other kinds of herbaceous wild-flower species in the park are known to have been eaten, uprooted, or trampled. Wild boars also damage tree roots and seedlings, but apparently avoid beeches, thus favoring the root sprouting of this species. They root up grass sod on balds, which speeds the invasion of balds by other herbaceous plants and trees and they cause soil erosion by removing the plant cover. They also harm native species by preying on those mentioned above and destroying the nests and eggs of ground-nesting birds such as grouse and turkeys.

With such a list of black marks against the non-native wild boar, it becomes readily apparent why the National Park Service is concerned about its numbers in the park. Conventional methods of trapping and directly reducing the boar population have limited their impact in certain areas of the park. Unfortunately, because of the animal's tremendous reproductive capability the efforts are not successful in reducing the total park population. The technology to completely eradicate the boar from the park is not available at the present time. Park Service research is now aimed at control methods. Estimates of the boar population have ranged upward to 2,000. But no reliable method of counting the boar in the park has yet been devised. University of Tennessee research has indicated that there may be at least 1,000 boars in the national park. Other estimates suggest there might be twice that many. Wild boars can reproduce any month of the year and most females bear a litter of from one to twelve piglets each year. And the wild boar has few enemies in the park, although bears and bobcats may occasionally take the young boars. With such a high reproductive potential, and so few controlling agents, the wild boar population has reached a size that severely alters and damages the park's natural environment.

Contrast these population dynamics with those of a competing native species, the black bear: Bears reproduce every other year, typically giving birth to only two cubs. When the mast fails they may not reproduce at all, apparently because the embryo does not implant, or is resorbed, or the mother has insufficient milk to keep the young alive. In some years, when bears wander out of the national park, many are killed by hunters. Each year poaching within the park takes several more. Hunting aside, bear populations became attuned to the supportive capacity of the environment through centuries of adaptation. Wild boars have been here only a few decades, far too short a time for the species to be integrated into the total forest community.

As the wild boars multiply unchecked in the park, they damage ground cover, inhibit tree reproduction, increase erosion, and decrease the native animals with which they compete for food. Perhaps hardest hit are black bears, squirrels, and those other species that in the fall depend on the all-important acorn.

Boars

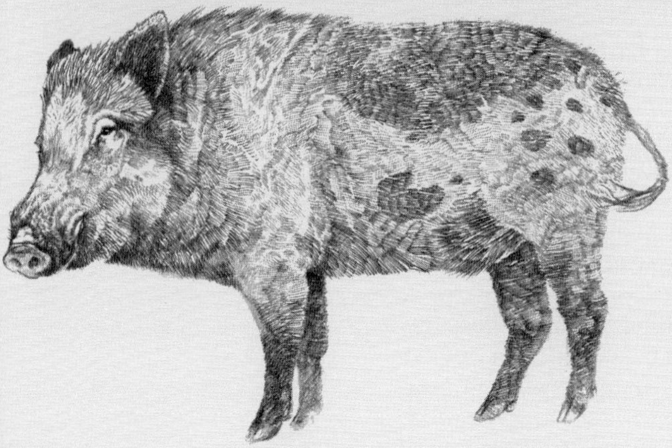

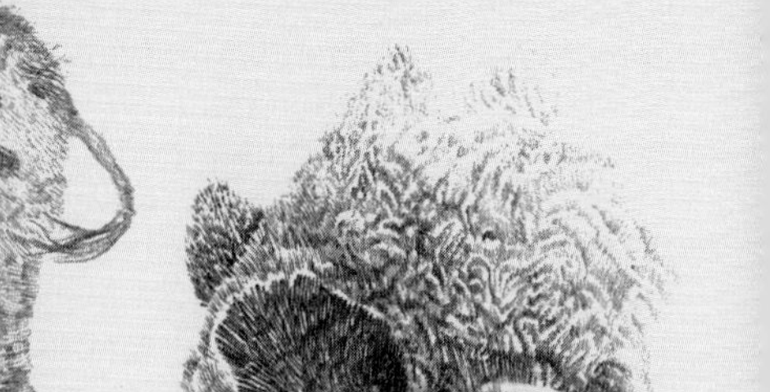

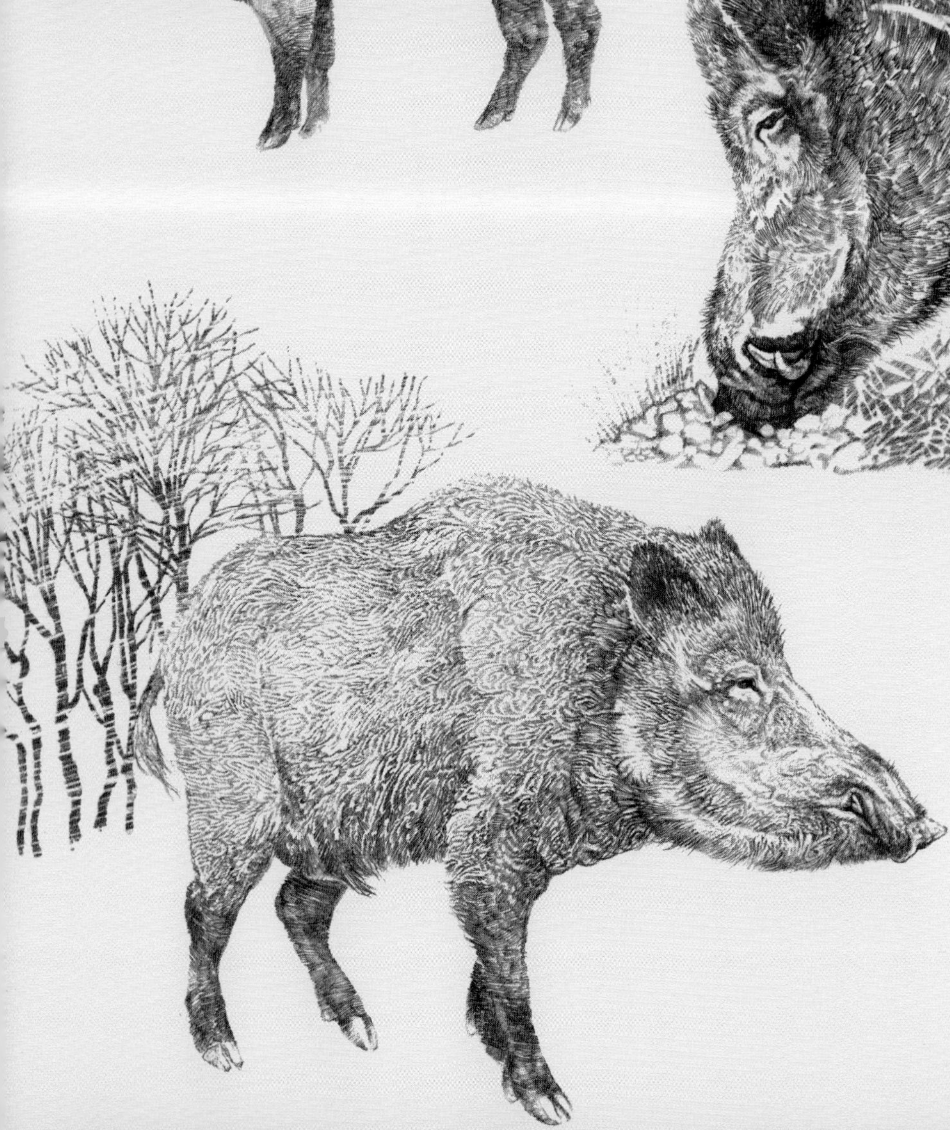

The wild boar came to the Great Smoky Mountains National Park uninvited in the early 1920s. While its population remained small, the boar was not thought a menace. Since the 1960s however, it has become obvious that the boar constitutes an ecological disaster of great proportions. In feeding, the animals move together and root up the ground or a stream bed with unbelievable thoroughness.

After boars have tackled a stretch of trout stream, it looks as though a bulldozer had churned it up. Presumably they seek aquatic insects, salamanders, and even a few small fish. Salamanders are among the park's chief biological treasures, so the boars have not endeared themselves to those who are responsible for managing wildlife here in the park.

Another biological prize in these mountains is the grass bald habitat. These energetic porkers were not slow to find balds a food source, ravenously digging for June beetle larvae. The grass bald survives only by the turf's resistance to tree invasions, so the boar and its plowing threatens the existence of these unique, and as yet incompletely understood, grass balds that are both prizes and puzzles.

Over the years it has been suggested that diverse species are directly threatened by the expanding boar population. These include ground-nesting birds, yellow adder's-tongue and other wildflowers, and possibly deer and bear.

Studies are underway to determine the extent of the boar's damage, and hence the real threat they pose. But we have no good comparative figures on the populations of other species for the years before boars arrived. Despite this lack, it has not been difficult to brand the boar a villain. But to control them has not been so easy. In good years they thrive—and gobble up more park resources.

There is a food preference relationship between turkeys, deer, bear, and boars in their mutual dependence on annual acorn and hickory nut crops. The widespread chestnut blight wiped out this dependable annual crop of nuts on which bears, deer, turkeys, and other animals fed in preparation for winter before the boars arrived. Now all these species compete— and the prolific boar is a lusty competitor—for a more uncertain acorn/hickory crop.

Some would cast the boar as pure villain. Others would say that people are at fault for introducing the boar into this region as an exotic species. The sport of hunting was anticipated with relish but the consequences were not considered at all. The boars have now bred with domestic pigs to such an extent that the markings vary from animal to animal. Some show definite spots, others few or none at all. Wildlife artist George Founds, who drew the boars and bear on these pages, was once a guide in this region.

The woodlands rooting of the boars is impossible to miss at trailside. A person could not do as well with ax and hoe—or power tiller!

The wild boar is winning the contest with park efforts to control it. Fewer than 200 are trapped or killed in a year, and even these are soon replaced by the boar's high reproductive capabilities.

Piglets are born nearly naked, so the mother builds a nest for their first week of life.

Many admire the bear above all other park animals, associating it intimately with wilderness scenery. Not seeing a bear can be a disappointment. But bears are shy and secretive; about 95 percent never come near the roads here. You might be surprised that bears, classed as carnivores, are about 80 percent vegetarian. But they will eat almost anything.

The sow will usually have two cubs every two years. They are born blind and hairless, no bigger than a young rabbit. In two months they will leave the den under the watchful, if indulgent, eye of a fiercely protective mother who is a stern disciplinarian. It is good training, for bears live by stealth and cunning as much as brute strength. (Scientists think bears may be almost as bright as primates.) Bears feed in summer on berries. In autumn they forage on hickory nuts and acorns to build fat reserves for the long winter they spend in the den.

Bears are tree climbers (see note on denning below), especially if climbing brings food within reach. Bears have been observed bending small trees double. Many they will break to get at the fruit. They may climb out on branches to get at fruit, or break the branches off and consume the fruit on the ground.

The relationship of a mother bear and her cubs can be fascinating to watch. Even hard-nosed biologists must quell the urge to describe this relationship in purely human terms! The relationship is best watched at a distance, however, because the mother is fiercely protective of her young. That protective instinct can prove dangerous for the unwary hiker or backpacker. Generally, however, bears will sense you first and avoid you entirely.

Cubs develop their strength and coordination in tumbling games of tag and wrestling. A cub is full grown at age 4. A bear is old by age 12. The park's bear population varies from about 400 to 600.

A few years ago it was discovered here in the Smokies that bear denning sites are frequently in hollow trees 6 to 15 meters (20 to 50 feet) above the ground. Holes near the ground (photo) are not commonly used.

The intelligence of bears is often underrated. They seem to walk awkwardly, because their hindquarters are longer than their forelimbs, but they are agile and move rapidly.

The Tracks of Our Predecessors

Rocks rose out of the sea and became mountains. Plants clothed them and animals lived among the plants, all evolving and changing over the millions of years. A few thousand years ago, a dense green mantle of giant trees covered the Smokies. Bears roamed the forest and bison followed their ages-old trails across the mountains. Beavers built dams across lowland streams, and meadows followed when the beavers moved on. Elk and deer came out of the forest to feed in the meadows and cougars and wolves hunted the elk and deer. It might have gone on this way for even more thousands of years.

But then people came. First Indians, then settlers, then the lumber companies. What was the impact of this new element, this two-legged animal? How did the forest and its life change? Is it now returning to its former state? In trying to answer these questions we may learn something about the ecological role of people not only in the Smokies but also in much of eastern North America, most of which resembled the Smokies in its forest cover when people first arrived on the scene.

For at least several thousand years groups of humans have lived in the lowlands around the Great Smokies. Use of the highlands themselves by these earlier groups was probably limited, however. Our history of peoples in the mountains begins with reports of explorers who visited the Cherokees in the late 17th and 18th centuries. They found this tribe, which is thought to have left the ancestral Iroquoian territory and moved southward about the year 1000, dispersed in small villages along foothill streams in a great arc around the Southern Appalachians. Primarily an agricultural people, the Cherokees tended fields of corn, squash, beans, melons, and tobacco around their thatched log cabins. But they also hunted and fished, and gathered wild plant materials for both food and trade. Although the mountains harbored spirits that were not entirely friendly, the Cherokees camped in coves and gaps to hunt bear and deer, to gather nuts and berries, and to gather stone for implements. Early reports from the Smokies noted the large numbers of deer, bear, and beaver skins being traded by the Cherokees. Quite possibly, they set fire to attract game and promote the growth of berry bushes, thus creating some of the myste-

Imagine hewing your own home out of the surrounding woodlands with just a few hand tools. Such was the life of Smokies pioneers. Today you can peer into the past at the Pioneer Farmstead beside the Oconaluftee Visitor Center.

rious grass balds atop the Smokies. For purposes of trade and warfare they established trails through the mountains. Such a trail across Indian Gap remained the principal cross-mountain route until early this century.

What effect did all this have on the tapestry of life in the mountains? Undoubtedly the Cherokees increased the area of open land, although some of their cropland might have been established on old beaver meadows. They may also have reduced the numbers of game and fur animals, although 18th-century travelers in the region still could be amazed at the abundance of deer, bison, beaver, cougars, and other animals. No species except the bison is known to have disappeared during the years the Cherokees had sole dominion over the land, and they may have contributed in some way to this one loss. With relatively small numbers in the Smokies, and a lack of highly destructive implements, especially guns, the Cherokees apparently changed the ecological picture only slightly in the days before contact with Europeans.

In the 1790s settlers, legally or illegally, began taking over former Cherokee land in the Smokies, beginning with two of the broader lowland valleys, the Oconaluftee and Cades Cove. As the Cherokees yielded more and more land, by treaty or to theft, settlement by the new Americans proceeded up other valleys, until by 1826 almost every watershed was occupied by at least a few families. Clearing and occupation of land continued through the 19th century, the largest concentrations developing in the Sugarlands (along the West Prong of Little Pigeon River), Greenbrier Cove, and Cataloochee, in addition to the earliest areas of settlement. In 1926, when land buying for the newly authorized park began, there were 1,200 farms and 7,300 people within the park boundaries. By this time, however, farming in the Smokies had passed its peak.

By contrast with earlier Indian inhabitants, the farmers had considerable impact on the land. Most obvious was the removal of forest to make homesites, cropland, and pastures. By 1902, eight percent of the land on the Tennessee side of the Smokies and seven percent on the North Carolina side had been cleared. As settlement proceeded up a hollow farmers were confronted with steeper and steeper slopes. The inevitable results of trying to raise corn on the sides of mountains were rapid loss of fertility and then of the soil itself, as the heavy rains leached out nutrients and washed away first the humus and then the mineral soil beneath. In this wilderness where virgin land was still abundant, many mountaineers simply cleared a new patch when the old one gave out. Horace Kephart, a midwesterner who lived among such farmers on the North Carolina side early in the 20th century, recorded their approach to cultivation. They would clear land and get out two or three crops of corn.

"When corn won't grow no more I can turn the field into grass a couple o' years," Kephart's informant says.

"Then you'll rotate, and grow corn again?" Kephart asks, a bit ingenuously.

"La, no! By that time the land will be so poor hit wouldn't raise a cuss-fight."

"But then you must move, and begin all over again." Kephart counters. "This continual moving must be a great nuisance."

Kephart overstates the case, however, because most stayed in one house for two to three generations, or about 50 to 75 years.

Clearing and the erosion that sometimes followed were relatively local and distinct effects of settlement. Uses of uncleared forest land had widespread, but more subtle, effects. Selected white pines and yellow-poplars were cut for lumber; oaks for shingles; and hickories mostly for firewood. Other species were put to less important, miscellaneous uses. Many plants were collected for food and dyes or for medicinal purposes. Ginseng, which has a forked root highly prized in China for its supposed medicinal and aphrodisiac values, was nearly eliminated by eager "sang" diggers who sold the roots for export. Probably even more pervasive was the influence of livestock. Hogs, and sometimes cattle and sheep, were allowed to roam the forests, grazing, browsing, and rooting for a living. Mast—acorns, chestnuts, and beechnuts—formed an important part of the diet of hogs, but these omnivorous creatures ate all sorts of plants and small animals. As anyone knows who has observed a grazed woodlot, livestock can quickly impoverish the ground and shrub layers of a forest. Grazing and browsing, along with use of fire, prevented the return of forest to the grass balds. All these uses of the forest undoubtedly changed the proportions of many tree and lesser plant species in the total forest composition. Precisely how much they did so cannot now be determined.

The impact of settlement on certain wildlife species is more easily seen. Elk disappeared about the time the earliest pioneers moved in. The beaver, an easily trapped animal, was nearly gone by the end of the 19th century. Wolves and cougars, hunted because they sometimes killed livestock—and uncomfortable in the presence of people—followed soon after. Deer, bear, and turkey persisted but in much-reduced numbers, with the bears retreating to rough, wild country in the central heights. Smaller animals fared better, although such hunted species as raccoon, opossum, and gray squirrel perhaps suffered some reduction.

About 1900 a new era began, bringing the greatest shock yet to Great Smokies ecosystems. Large lumber companies, having logged off the big timber of New England and the Great Lakes states, turned their attention to the virgin stands of the Southern Appalachians. Setting up sawmills at the fringes of the mountains, they rapidly worked their way up the coves, just as Cherokees and settlers had done before them. Railroads, built to carry logs to the mills, were extended upstream as cutting progressed. In some watersheds, such as those of the Little River, Big Creek, and the Oconaluftee, nearly all species of trees were taken. In others, such as Abrams Creek, West Prong of the Little Pigeon, and Cataloochee, cutting was selective. By the late 1920s, logging, added to settlement practices, had at least partially cleared more than 60 percent of the land in the Great Smoky Mountains.

Though for a time it proved an economic boon, logging was easily the most destructive form of land use the region was ever subjected to. The removal of forest cover and the skidding of logs down steep mountainsides caused widespread erosion. This weakened the foundation for regrowth and clogged streams with sediment, thereby reducing their quality for sustaining aquatic life. In the wake of logging came forest fires, probably the worst these mountains have seen. Heaps of dried branches trimmed from logs made perfect tinder for fires started by engine sparks, careless matches, or lightning strikes. In the 1920s disastrous fires roared up the East Prong of Little River, up Forney Creek to Clingmans Dome, and over the slopes around Charlies Bunion. Scars from some of these fires have still not healed today.

What was the net biological effect of the presence of people in the mountains in 1926, the year Congress authorized Great Smoky Mountains National Park? Broadly speaking, the forest and its animals had been diminished but the plants and animals of grassland and brush had increased. The gray wolf was gone but the meadowlark had arrived. In 1930 the American people inherited lands that were still about 40 percent virgin forest, the largest such chunk of forest left in the East. The rest of the park was a patchwork of uncut forest, young second growth, and openings dotted with houses and barns and fringed with stone walls and fences. The park therefore preserved much of the primeval splendor of the Smokies, but the activities of people would long remain visible in it, and some of these would deliberately be maintained as part of the region's historical heritage.

Today most of the former fields, except those such as Cades Cove that are purposely kept open, have returned to forest. But it is still easy to recognize these grown-over fields by the types of trees on them. Many bear a nearly solid stand of straight-stemmed yellow-poplars. Others are marked by a dense growth of pines. Dr. Randolph Shields, who grew up in Cades Cove and became chairman of the biology department at nearby Maryville College, has watched the plant succession on old fields in the Cove since about 1930. He has found there that pines usually are the first trees to spring up among the grasses, herbs, and blackberries and other shrubs that follow field abandonment. On moist ground, yellow-poplars usually come up under the pines, but sometimes hemlock and white pine form a second tree stage under the pioneering Virginia or pitch pines. Where yellow-poplars come in, they usually shade out the light-loving pines in about 40 years. Gradually the many species of the cove forest become established under the yellow-poplars, presaging the mixed stand of big trees that will complete the cycle initiated by clearing the land. On the drier slopes it may take about 100 years for the pines to be shaded out by the red maples, oaks, and hickories that eventually become dominant in such areas.

As you might expect, animal life changes with the progression of plant succession. Meadowlarks, bobwhites, woodchucks, and cottontails are replaced by red-eyed vireos, wood thrushes, chipmunks, and white-footed mice as grassland and shrubs give way to forest. With age and woodpecker activity, tree cavities develop in the forest, providing homes for an additional complement of animals such as screech owls, flying squirrels, raccoons, bears, and opossums.

Under the protection accorded by its designation as a national park several animals have made a dramatic comeback in the Smokies. Bears once again roam the entire mountain area. Turkeys are frequently seen in such places as Cades Cove, where openings break the mantle of forest. In recent years sporadic beaver activity has been noted in the park. Even cougars are occasionally reported, although their presence has not been conclusively established. But wolves, elk, and bison—animals that symbolize the Indian's America—probably cannot be brought back.

Nature again reigns supreme in the Smokies. We may never see here the numbers of wildlife that surprised the first explorers, but we can see remnants of the giant-treed forests that greeted them, and we can marvel at the undulating expanse of green, a beautiful suggestion of the vast hardwood forest that once cloaked eastern America.

A great part of the Great Smokies story is the story of men and women making their homes in these wooded eastern mountains. With few tools and even fewer manufactured fixtures and fasteners, pioneers settled in and became mountaineers.

Industry—hard work, that is—and ingenuity came in handy. Many aspects of these traits are illustrated in this section through historic photographs of men and women going about their business in the Smokies. It was not all hard work, but even the play often exhibited these folk's ingenuity in turning the things of field and forest into implements of recreation.

For more insight into the lives of Smokies people, see the National Park Service book, *Highland Homeland: The People of the Great Smokies,* by Wilma Dykeman and Jim Stokely. It is sold in the park visitor centers and by mail (see "Armchair Explorations" on page 125).

Preceding page: Milas Messer dresses or curries a hide in the drying shed at his farm on Cove Creek.

Fitting barrel to stock

Chiseling a tub mill wheel

Coopering

Interior of a mill

Rolling sorghum cane

Hauling wood

Repairing a hauling sled

Beekeeping

Splitting shingles

Hog butchering

Scrubbing a hide

Shaving barrel staves

88

Gunsmithing

Basket weaving

Blacksmithing

89

Churning butter

Ginning cotton

Carding wool

Making baskets

Weaving yarn into cloth

Wash day

Oconaluftee

What kind of people were the Smokies pioneers? Part of the answer awaits you at the Pioneer Farmstead next to the Oconaluftee Visitor Center on the North Carolina side of the park. The farmstead buildings suggest an independent people who were hardworking, laboring spring, summer, and fall to prepare for the coming winter.

This is a typical Southern Appalachian pioneer farm. The life style of earlier years is demonstrated by people in period dress here from May through October. A few animals roam the farmyard and the garden produces traditional crops. In the fall sorghum cane may be pressed to make sorghum molasses. Inside the cabin—you can poke your head through its open doors and windows—traditional breads may be baking, or a quilt be patching, or wool a-spinning. And don't forget to notice the fieldstone chimneys, the squared logs' careful notchings, and the handsplit wooden "shakes" up on the roof.

Just up the road is Mingus Mill, an excellent example of a turbine-powered gristmill. A

stones used for grinding corn were cut domestically.

A commercial mill the size of Mingus Mill would generally be built by a specially skilled carpenter known as a millwright, a term which has taken broader meaning today.

miller is often on hand May through October to answer your questions about how waterpower was used to produce cornmeal and flour. You might even be able to purchase some of the cornmeal or the flour ground right at the mill. Wheat is harder than corn and requires harder stone to grind it. Millstones for grinding wheat in this area were imported from France. The

Cades Cove

Cades Cove preserves the image of the early settlers' self-sufficient life style in the Smokies. It was not all romance. Cades Cove itself is expansive, level, idyllic farmland, which hardly describes most of the Smokies. Cades Cove is today an open air museum. Here are the beautifully restored and picturesque Elijah Oliver cabin; the still-operated Cable Mill grinding flour with water power; and numerous churches, houses, and cabins. At Cable Mill are many

artifacts of past agricultural practices from throughout the Smokies. The largely self-sufficient agricultural economy here came to an end with the advent of logging about 1900.

By 1920, most Smokies residents were linked to a cash economy, to manufactured items and store-bought foods. But Cades Cove preserves glimpses of the pioneer ingenuity that wrested

a living from the landscape. Preserved with the cabins here are many ingenious devices such as effective door latches simply fashioned from local wood.

In 1850 Cades Cove supported 685 people in 132 families. Most originally came from Virginia via routes followed today by Interstate 81 and U.S. 411. A treaty in 1819 transferred the Cades Cove from Cherokee to State of Tennessee ownership. Settlers traded in what is now Townsend, and in Maryville and Knoxville.

A delightful 18-kilometer (11-mile) one-way loop road unfolds the quiet pleasures of Cades Cove to you. This is a popular route with bikers because it is so scenic—and not so arduous. Periodically the loop road is closed to motor vehicles for the sake of bicyclists. Early farmers were quick to appreciate the same level aspect of the cove that appeals to today's cyclist.

Cherokee Indians

The Cherokee nation was settled in the shadow of the Smokies. "The place of the blue smoke," they called the mountains in their heartland, and so the Smokies have become named. Myth, ritual, and religion bound the Cherokees closely to the land. Ironically, they enjoyed a sophisticated culture very similar to the white culture that would so cruelly supplant them. They were agrarian and democratic, and they believed in one god. They lived in mud-and-log cabins, women

sharing tribal governance, and men sharing household duties.

The Cherokees rapidly adopted governmental features of the invading culture. They adopted

a written legal code in 1808. Within a dozen years they had divided their nation into judicial districts with designated judges. Two years later they had established the Supreme Court of the

Cherokees; by 1827 they had their own constitution.

The design of an entire alphabet for the Cherokee language, by Sequoia, marked an unparalleled feat. Within just two years of its adoption, *The Cherokee Phoenix* newspaper was published and most Cherokee-speakers could read and write! But the white people had an insatiable appetite for land. Treaty after treaty was made and broken. The final blow was the discovery of gold in 1828 near the Cherokee villages in northern Georgia. Within a few years all their land was confiscated. The infamous "Trail of Tears" came with passage of the 1830 Removal Act.

Some 13,000 Cherokees were forced to march to Oklahoma; 25 percent died en route. Not all left, however, and some soon returned. Today the eastern band of Cherokees lives on the Cherokee Reservation on the park's North Carolina side.

3

Guide and Adviser

Going to the Great Smokies

The Great Smoky Mountains National Park straddles the North Carolina-Tennessee boundary for about 110 kilometers (70 miles). It is accessible by car from the Interstate highways encircling it as they connect the Tennessee cities of Knoxville and Chattanooga with Asheville, North Carolina; Greenville, South Carolina; and Atlanta, Georgia. The Blue Ridge Parkway reaches its southern terminus here on the park's North Carolina side. Major gateways to the park are Cherokee and Bryson City, North Carolina, and the cities of Pigeon Forge, Gatlinburg, Townsend, and Cosby, in Tennessee. These urban areas with their tourist services are connected by Newfound Gap Road (U.S. 441), the only park road that crosses the mountains. It is closed to commercial vehicles.

The National Park Service, U.S. Department of the Interior, is responsible for the management of the park. The superintendent's address is Gatlinburg, Tennessee 37738. Telephone (615) 436-5615. Park headquarters is located 3.2 kilometers (2 miles) south of Gatlinburg, on the Newfound Gap Road.

Maps, guides, and information on routes, points of interest, accommodations, and services are available from several sources. For a Tennessee highway map write to the Department of Transportation, Nashville, Tennessee 37243-0349, or telephone (615) 741-2331. For Tennessee vacation information write to Department of Tourist Development, P.O. Box 23170, Nashville, Tennessee 37202, or telephone (615) 741-2158. For a North Carolina highway map write to Travel and Tourism Division, 430 No. Salisbury, Raleigh, North Carolina 27603, or telephone (919) 733-4171.

A low sun casts fencepost shadows on a Cades Cove road. The relatively flat cove was premium farmland. Geologically, the cove floor is limestone, younger than the rocks forming surrounding ridges. The Rich Mountain mass skidded across what is now the cove as the Smokies range was being formed. Previous pages: The Cades Cove loop drive is reserved for bicyclists certain hours each week. Its level demeanor looks like heaven if you have biked across the mountains.

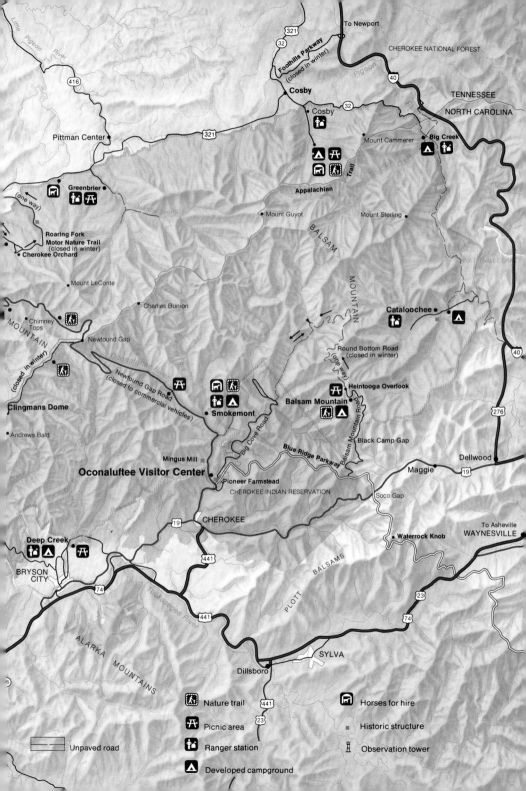

Little Pigeon River

(416)

To Newport

321

32 Foothills Parkway (closed in winter)

CHEROKEE NATIONAL FOREST

40

Cosby

Cosby

32

TENNESSEE
NORTH CAROLINA

Pittman Center

321

Mount Cammerer

Big Creek

Greenbrier

(one way)

Appalachian Trail

Roaring Fork
Motor Nature Trail
(closed in winter)
Cherokee Orchard

Mount Guyot

Mount Sterling

Mount LeConte

BALSAM

MOUNTAIN

Cataloochee

MOUNTAIN

Chimney Tops

Charlies Bunion

Newfound Gap

Round Bottom Road
(closed in winter)

40

276

(closed in winter)

Newfound Gap Road
(closed to commercial vehicles)

Clingmans Dome

Smokemont

(one way)

Heintooga Overlook

Balsam Mountain

Andrews Bald

Big Cove Road

Balsam Mountain Road

Black Camp Gap

Dellwood

Mingus Mill

Blue Ridge Parkway

Maggie

19

Oconaluftee Visitor Center

Pioneer Farmstead

CHEROKEE INDIAN RESERVATION

Soco Gap

CHEROKEE

19

Waterrock Knob

To Asheville
WAYNESVILLE

Deep Creek

BALSAMS

BRYSON CITY

441

74

PLOTT

23

Tuckasegee River

441

74

ALARKA MOUNTAINS

SYLVA

Dillsboro

441

23

Nature trail

Picnic area

Ranger station

Unpaved road

Developed campground

Horses for hire

Historic structure

Observation tower

The division distributes several brochures on North Carolina vacations, recreation, and special events; specify your interest in the Smokies. The *North Carolina Outdoors* booklet lists areas and facilities, including private campgrounds, keyed to the official highway map.

Chambers of commerce offer trip information: Pigeon Forge Chamber of Commerce, P.O. Box 1390, Pigeon Forge, Tennessee 37868; telephone 800-251-9100 or (615) 453-8574. Gatlinburg Chamber of Commerce, P.O. Box 527, Gatlinburg, Tennessee 37738; telephone 800-822-1998 or (615) 436-4178. Townsend Chamber of Commerce, Townsend, Tennessee 37882. Cosby Chamber of Commerce, Cosby, Tennessee 37722. Cherokee Chamber of Commerce, P.O. Box 460, Cherokee, North Carolina 28719; telephone (704) 497-9195. Bryson City Chamber of Commerce, Bryson City, North Carolina 28713; (704) 488-3681. Lodging and supplies are available in Pigeon Forge, Gatlinburg, Sevierville, Townsend, Maryville, Bryson City, Cherokee, and other Tennessee and North Carolina towns surrounding the park. No public transportation serves the national park. Major airlines serve Knoxville, Tennessee and Asheville, North Carolina, where cars may be rented.

Visitor Centers

National Park Service Visitor Centers are located just inside the park on both the North Carolina and Tennessee sides. On the Tennessee side the Sugarlands Visitor Center is 3.2 kilometers (2 miles) south of Gatlinburg. The Cades Cove Visitor Center (closed in winter) is located in the Cable Mill area of the Cades Cove Loop Road. On the North Carolina side the Oconaluftee Visitor Center is 3.2 kilometers (2 miles) north of Cherokee.

If you plan to be in the park just a few hours or up to several days, you will do yourself a favor by checking out a visitor center. Museum displays give you a quick and interesting insight into both nature and history in the park. At Sugarlands there is a free movie. Books, maps, and other publications are offered for sale in the visitor centers and free park folders are available. These resources—and the people working the information desks—can help you plan your stay in the park within the time limits you must meet.

The Great Smokies is a large park whose diverse features are separated by significant driving times. Park employees can help you use your time to best advantage.

Visitor centers also offer restroom facilities, drinking water, and a mail drop and they sell film for your convenience. Here you can get backpacking information and apply for a backcountry use permit. (See section on Backcountry Use.) Visitor center bulletin boards carry information on road conditions, urgent contact requests, and interpretive programs.

Visitor centers are open 8 a.m. to 4:30 p.m. during the winter, with extended hours of operation in the spring, summer, and fall. The Cades Cove Visitor Center is open from 9 a.m. to 5 p.m. from mid-April to late November.

Interpretive Programs

Guided walks and evening programs are conducted by the National Park Service throughout the park. Most of these start or take place at the visitor centers and at campground amphitheaters. The uniformed park employees who render these services are trained in the natural history and/or history of the Great Smokies. They give you excellent vignettes of the park's nature and its historical period of Indian

Sugarlands Visitor Center (top) in Tennessee and Oconaluftee Visitor Center in North Carolina, are the best places to begin your park trip. Exhibits explain the natural and human history of the Great Smokies. A free park folder is available, books and maps are sold, and you can check the posted schedule of activities being offered.

and mountaineer life and the opportunity to ask questions. You, for instance, might enjoy a short nature walk up a burbling Smokies stream and so learn about the more than 1,100 kilometers (700 miles) of streams in the park. Schedules of these activities and programs are posted at the visitor centers and on campground bulletin boards. A copy of the schedule is in *Guide to Great Smoky Mountains National Park,* which is available free at any visitor center, ranger station, or campground.

Live demonstrations of mountain life skills and folkways are also provided periodically (spring through October) at places such as the Pioneer Farmstead beside the Oconaluftee Visitor Center and the nearby Mingus Mill, or at the Cable Mill in Cades Cove. You even might be able to buy cornmeal freshly ground just as it was a century or more ago.

Self-guiding nature trails have been laid out throughout the park. Look for these marked trails near campgrounds, visitor centers, and picnic areas. Most are easy walks of 1.5 kilometers (a mile) or less which take you through former farmsteads now returning to forest, groves of the world-famous cove hardwoods, reclaimed logged-over lands, or other aspects of the park. Trails are well marked and seldom difficult. At the trail's start look for a container offering a descriptive brochure for sale on the honor system.

Two self-guiding motor nature trails lead you through impressive areas of the park in the comfort and convenience of your own vehicle. Near Gatlinburg, off the Cherokee Orchard Road, is the Roaring Fork Motor Nature Trail. Its scenic route takes you by several restored pioneer buildings. The Cades Cove Loop Road is an 18-kilometer (11-mile) drive through the pleasant scenery of Cades Cove. Here you get pleasant vistas out across the cove where you may well see deer grazing against a mountain backdrop. The fields recall the rural scene of many years ago. A brochure available at the start of the loop describes points along the way that are designated by numbered signs. At several points you can park your car and visit preserved farm structures, both log and frame, and churches and cemeteries. Partway through the loop is a small visitor center and the restored Cable Mill. Associated restored buildings here display farm implements once used for valley and mountain farming in this region.

Guided interpretive programs are offered largely in summer. Check the current schedule at the visitor centers or on campground bulletin boards.

Evening campground programs offer interesting free family entertainment. Try the many interpretive programs offered at park campgrounds in the evenings throughout the week. Check bulletin boards for the schedules.

The three most often asked questions in the park are: Where can I fish? Where can I camp? and What about the bears? Some evening programs cover the bears in detail and you will learn about unusual denning habits in the Smokies. All evening programs are offered for the general public by trained National Park Service interpreters. You will enjoy them no matter how much, or how little, you know about the topic. And you are free to ask questions, knowing they will be taken seriously.

Evening programs cover such topics as the pioneer life, wildlife, hiking, and the incredible botanical story of the Smokies. There are programs on the "preserve and protect" philosophy of how the park is managed, and exploring the park. For the adventurous there are "night prowls," guided experiences after dark to sample the sights, sounds, and odors of the night forest.

Quiet walkways provide short walks on easy grades. They usually begin at parking areas that accommodate no more than two cars, so crowds are excluded. This is a nice way to experience the naturalness of the Smokies in walks not exceeding 0.5 kilometers (0.3 miles).

They still grind corn sometimes by the old water-driven methods at the restored Mingus Mill (top), just up the road from the Oconaluftee Visitor Center. But school's in session at Little Greenbrier only for the sake of people who come to the park to see what life was like in the Smokies a couple of generations back. These living history demonstrations are sometimes offered in summer at various parts of the park. Check schedules at a visitor center or campground.

The Smokies by Car

A few comments may save time and open new vistas for your driving in the Smokies. Within just an hour's drive of each other here are climatic differences created by elevation. You can drive through the spruce-fir forests typical of Maine up near Clingmans Dome in late morning and be driving through lush southern hardwoods back near Sugarlands or Oconaluftee in early afternoon.

The roads are designed for scenic driving. There are numerous turnouts and parking areas at viewpoints or historic sites.

Traffic, winding roads, and the scenery conspire to making driving time more important than distance here in the park. Figure about twice the time to drive a given distance that you would for normal highways. Be on the alert for unexpected driving behavior from others—they may be under the influence of the scenery! Gasoline is not sold in the park, so check your gauge. Remember that winter storms may close the Newfound Gap and Little River Roads.

The main road in the park is the New-found Gap Road (U.S. 441) between Gatlinburg and Cherokee. It is the only road across the mountains. Along it and at the Newfound Gap Parking Area you will get some of the best scenic high-mountain vistas in the park—and on the East Coast, for that matter. If you want to go still higher you can drive up the Clingmans Dome Road from Newfound Gap and walk up to the observation tower. Here you are at the highest point in the national park, and the third highest east of the Rockies. The reward is a 360-degree panorama of the sea of peaks for which the Smokies (and Natahalas and Unakas and . . .) are famous. Clingmans Dome

Road is a deadend spur off the Newfound Gap Road at the crest of the Smokies.

If you want to sample the Blue Ridge Parkway and also enjoy some beautiful mountain scenery from right up in it, try the Balsam Mountain Road, which leaves the parkway between Oconaluftee and Soco Gap. It winds for 14.5 kilometers (9 miles) back into the national park's Balsam Mountain Campground. Incredible azalea displays will dazzle you here in season. If you are adventurous and want to try a mountain dirt road, continue past the campground to the Heintooga Picnic Area and the start of the Round Bottom Road (closed during winter). This is a 22.5-kilometer (14-mile), partially one-way, unpaved road that descends the mountain to the river valley below and joins the Big Cove Road in the Cherokee Indian Reservation. You come out right below Oconaluftee at the edge of the park.

Another view of the Smokies awaits you along the Little River Road leading from Sugarlands to Cades Cove. The road lies on the old logging railroad bed for a distance along the Little River. (The curves suggest these were not fast trains!) Spur roads lead off to Elkmont and Tremont deeper in the park, and to Townsend and Wear Cove, towns outside the park. Little River Road becomes the Laurel Creek Road and takes you on into Cades Cove where you can take the one-way 18-kilometer (11-mile) loop drive and observe the historic mountain setting of early settlers. If you are returning to Gatlinburg or Pigeon Forge from Cades Cove, try exiting the park toward Townsend and driving the beautiful Wear Cove Road back to U.S. 441 at the north end of Pigeon Forge.

Perhaps the most bucolic scenes in the Smokies are to be seen from the Foothills Parkway between Interstate 40 and Route 32 near Cosby, around the northeast tip of the park. Here you look out across beautiful farmland with the whole mass of the Smokies rising as its backdrop.

Other interesting drives in the park are the Rich Mountain Road, Parsons Branch Road (both closed in winter), and the Roaring Fork Motor Nature Trail. At the west end of the park there is another section of the Foothills Parkway between Chilhowee and Walland. The parkway is administered by the National Park Service. A small leaflet, "Auto Touring," is available for a small charge at any of the three visitor centers.

Mountain People and Folkways

Right beside the Oconaluftee Visitor Center as you enter the North Carolina side of the park is the Pioneer Farmstead, a restored small farm along the Oconaluftee River. As you leave the visitor center headed toward the mountains, Mingus Mill Parking Area soon appears on your left. The turbine-powered gristmill used water power to grind cornmeal and flour. Its millrace leaves a lively creek and spills toward the mill under arching mountain-laurel. Stones used to grind wheat came from France. Cornmeal stones were of local origin. Mingus Mill is open from May through October and a miller is usually on hand to answer your questions.

On the North Carolina side of the park limited restored structures are also found at Cataloochee.

The Cable Mill area in Cades Cove presents the largest group of restored structures on the Tennessee side of the park. Farming is still permitted in Cades Cove itself to preserve the open fields of the rural scene there. The 18-kilometer (11-mile) loop drive through Cades Cove takes you by numerous log and frame struc-

tures. The Elijah Oliver place is a particularly beautiful log structure with outbuildings in a cozy, shaded setting. The stream flowing through Elijah Oliver's springhouse once kept his milk supply cool.

Other pioneer structures include the Little Greenbrier School off Little River Road and cabins and houses along the Roaring Fork Motor Nature Trail. Close scrutiny of the many log structures shows subtle variations in notching and other details.

Living history demonstrations are offered in season at Cades Cove, Mingus Mill, and the Pioneer Farmstead. Check the visitor center and campground bulletin boards for schedules. These may include craft demonstrations and concerts of traditional mountain music. A "Mountain People" leaflet is available for a small charge at any of the park's visitor centers.

Preceding page: Ranger-led walks and evening campfire programs can be highlights of your park trip.

Wildflowers and Fall Colors

With abundant warm sunshine and frequent rainfall it is no surprise that about 200 species of showy wildflowers bloom in the Smokies. They begin in March and last until about November. Spring comes to mind when most of us think about flowers, but practically the whole year has something to offer. Spring seems to burst with flowers as they take advantage of good conditions for a short period between the cold of winter and the shade of summer, when full foliage blocks sunlight from the forest floor.

Bloom dates depend on the weather and can vary from year to year. Here are recommended dates to guide you: Dogwood and redbud, mid- to late-April; spring flowers, late March to mid-May; mountain-laurel and flame azalea, May and June; Catawba rhododendron, mid-June; and rosebay rhododendron, June and July.

Springtime flowers are trilliums, phacelia, violets, lady's-slippers, jack-in-the-pulpits, and showy orchis. There are familiar exotic (non-native) species too, such as the dandelion. (In the Smokies exotics are generally flowers of field and not of forest.) Goldenrod, ironweed, and asters bloom in late September to early October.

In August you may see wild clematis, yellow-fringed orchis, bee-balm, cardinal-flower, monkshood, and blue gentian.

Many flowers grow along park roadsides. Other good locations to see them are along quiet walkways and on designated nature trails throughout the park. See photographs of flowering shrubs and wildflowers on pages 58-61.

Fall colors generally peak between October 15 and 25. The presence of hardwood

species usually associated with more northerly climes makes the autumn leaves here the more spectacular. Up and down the mountain the brilliant reds of maples, the golden yellow of beech, and the deeper hues of oaks and more southerly species blend spectacularly. Fall color is the result of the breakdown of green chlorophyll in deciduous leaves. Yellow and brown pigments present all summer now become prominent. Red colors are produced when sugars are trapped in the sap of the leaves.

If you don't mind chilly nights this can be great camping weather, and a generally pleasant time of year here. Keep in mind that the traffic is particularly heavy in the park during the fall foliage season, especially on weekends.

A leaflet "Forests and Wildflowers" is available from any park visitor center for a small charge.

Spring and fall bursts of color are annual drawing cards in the Smokies. As the seasons progress, fall colors descend the mountains and spring colors "climb" upwards.

Activities

Horseback Riding

The park has many kilometers of horse trails and this is considered some of the finest riding country in the East. If you have your own horses and want to use them in the Smokies, write to the superintendent and request the "Great Smoky Mountains Trail Map" folder and other current information on horse use in the park. The folder provides basic information on sites and regulations and indicates horse trails. The regulations are designed to minimize the environmental impact of stock.

If you don't own a horse, don't worry. You can rent one from a concessioner by the hour, half day, day, or overnight at five locations in the park: Cades Cove, Cosby, Dudley Creek, Smokemont, and Sugarlands. The National Park Service requires the concessioner to send a guide with all horse parties; this service is included in the basic rental rate. For overnight trips you must bring your own food. Saddlebags and shelter are provided.

If you want to experience a more traditional "outfitted" horseback trip, write to area chambers of commerce for names of commercial outfitters.

Bicycling

The best place to bike in the Smokies is Cades Cove. If you don't arrive on your own bike or carry it on your car, you can rent one from the concessioner there, except in winter. The 18-kilometer (11-mile) loop road is a paved, generally level-to-rolling one-way country road around the cove. It takes you by restored pioneer and settlers' structures, both log and frame.

Along the way are many pleasant streams, hiking trail access points, wooded stretches,

Fishing Smokies streams and rivers and the nearby TVA lakes (top) is a popular pastime. Most sought after in the park are rainbow and brown trout. Pictured here is the brook trout. Please take a good look because possession of any brook trout is prohibited in the park.

and the Cable Mill area with a small visitor center. The scenery is nothing if not glorious. You look out across the rolling, open meadow to the mountains. And you may see herds of deer grazing. In summer bikers have the loop road to themselves—no cars allowed—on Saturday mornings until 10 a.m.

Biking conditions elsewhere in the park are not generally good. The Newfound Gap Road is steep, winding, crushingly long, and can be full of traffic. Other park roads tend to be winding and narrow as well.

The Cades Cove bicycle concession is located at the campground.

Fishing

The Smokies offer a chance to fish in rushing mountain streams and rivers. Of the 70 or so kinds of fish in the park, those that can be fished for are smallmouth bass, rock bass, and rainbow and brown trout. The native brook trout is protected and its waters are closed to fishing. Rainbows and brown trout are non-native species and are managed to provide sustained-yield fishing.

With a valid Tennessee or North Carolina license you may fish open park waters from sunrise to sunset. A license is required for all persons 13 years of age and older in Tennessee and 16 years of age and older in North Carolina. Buy licenses in nearby towns. Fishing with bait is prohibited. Only single-hook artificial lures may be used. Possession and size limits may vary with stream and species of fish, so check before you fish. In general, *the possession of any brook trout is prohibited.* The National Park Service hopes to restore some native brook trout waters encroached upon by introduced brown and rainbow trout.

Local regulations are posted on streams and can be obtained at any park ranger station or visitor center. Or write to the park superintendent in advance of your trip.

Birding the Smokies

The variety of birds here is striking. A one-day count throughout the park and vicinity in winter will net more than 50 species even in a bad year. More than 20 warblers are considered to breed within the park, and nearly 30 members of the finch family have been reported here. Geese and ducks number nearly 20 species, but are not often seen. Craggy mountain heights provide ideal habitat for ravens, some hawks, and occasional migrating peregrine falcons. Eagles and falcons are only occasionally, or rarely, seen, but the mere possibility is exciting. If you are interested in finding a particular bird or good birding places, check at a visitor center. Some birds are only seasonal residents or visitors of the park.

Serious birders will want to see a copy of the bird checklist. Free copies are available at visitor centers.

Hiking and Backpacking

A Hiker's Paradise

The fact that the National Park Service maintains 1,450 kilometers (900 miles) of trails says something about the Smokies and hiking: it's an East Coast hiker's paradise. Trails come in all lengths and levels of difficulty, for the handicapped, children, super-athletes, old folks, day hikers, and long-distance backpackers. The latter of course means the Appalachian Trail, which threads the Smokies crest on its way from Maine to Georgia. More on the AT below.

The intimacy of the Smokies wilderness surprises many who are attracted by the stunning mountain scenery. This intimacy, best seen afoot, is all but missed from your vehicle. So is the mood set by wildflowers, cascading streams, birdsong, and the fragrance of fir trees so startling in the Southeast. Hiking trails give access to waterfalls such as Juneywhank, Abrams, Hen Wallow, and Ramsay Cascades. A leaflet, "Streams and Waterfalls," is available at visitor centers for a small charge.

On sale at visitor centers you will find copies of the National Park Service's "Great Smoky Mountains Trail Map" folder. It has up-to-date information and a shaded relief map of trails and popular trailheads in the park. Detailed trail descriptions are found in the Sierra Club Totebook, *Hiker's Guide to the Smokies,* sold at visitor centers and in area book and outdoor equipment stores.

From mountain balds (top) to rocky canyon ledges, Smokies trails introduce you to aspects of the park invisible to motorists. Afoot, you experience the intimacy of natural detail that makes the Smokies internationally renowned.

You will want to wear comfortable, non-slip shoes whether you go out for a half-hour or a day. And you must expect variable weather, characteristic of the Smokies. Abundant rainfall can materialize quickly on a day which began so clear just hours ago. A light poncho or other rain gear is

114

All overnight camping except in established park campgrounds requires a free backcountry use permit (top). The permit system assures you and your party an appropriate measure of solitude in the backcountry. No matter where you camp in the park, you must be fully prepared for rainy weather.

handy. Make sure you will be warm enough, too. (See "Hypothermia Dangers" and "Winter Warnings.") Days that are warm at Sugarlands or Oconaluftee can be very cold if rain and wind catch you at higher elevations.

Attractions shift with the seasons in the Smokies. The best way to meld your own interests with current attractions for a pleasant hike is to seek advice at a visitor center. Describing your interests and asking "What's best to see this time of year?" may well produce custom-tailored hiking advice. You will notice hikes are described in time as well as distance because steeper trails make simple distance a deceptive measure. A leaflet, "Walks and Hikes," describes over 50 popular day hikes and is available from park visitor centers for a small charge.

Backcountry Use Permits

All overnight hiking in the park requires a backcountry use permit available free at visitor centers, and the Cades Cove campground kiosk. The permit system has as its purpose to protect the unspoiled character of the Smokies backcountry for the enjoyment of present and future users. Permits distribute use so that impact is not disproportionate in popular areas, and thus they provide backcountry users with an opportunity for increased solitude. You do not need a backcountry use permit for day hiking, only for overnight use. The "Great Smoky Mountains Trail Map" folder (see above) explains the permit system and its use. Information is also available at ranger stations or visitor centers. Or write: Backcountry Permit, in care of the park address; telephone (615) 436-1231 and ask for "Backcountry." You can reserve a specific backcountry campsite for one to three specific nights up to 30 days in advance under this permit system. You can do this in person, by telephone, or by mail. The permit itself must be picked up in person no earlier than 24 hours before the beginning of the trip. *Note:* Reservations for the entire trip are automatically canceled if your permit is not picked up by 12:00 noon on the first day of the scheduled trip. Permits will not be issued to groups larger than eight persons.

Competition for use of trail shelters along popular trails is great in the peak season. But you can pick and choose from among many uncrowded trails that offer trailside campsites. All water obtained in the backcountry should be boiled or chemically treated.

The Appalachian Trail

Of all the distance the Appalachian Trail spans between Maine and Georgia, perhaps no sustained portion is as virtually untouched by humanity as the 110 kilometers (70 miles) threading the crest of the Smokies. And this despite the fact that the overall trail is 3,244 kilometers (2,015 miles) long. You can park your car in the Newfound Gap Parking Area and walk the AT north or south for a pleasant walk—or day-long hike—along the Smokies crest. A popular destination to the north is Charlies Bunion. There, because of unrecovered fire openings on extremely steep mountain slopes, you achieve a real alpine sense and literal "peak" experience. You can also park below Clingmans Dome, a short spur drive south of Newfound Gap, and experience the AT.

About every 10-16 kilometers (8 to 10 miles) there are overnight shelters providing primitive bunks. These three-sided shelters are closed in on the fourth side with chainlink fence as bear-proofing. To stay in these shelters requires a backcountry use permit/reservation. Stays are limited to one night at a given shelter.

The Appalachian Trail traces 110 kilometers (70 miles) along the crest of the range. Overnight shelters (above) are screened against bears. Shelter use requires a backcountry use permit (see text). Through-hikers on the Appalachian Trail must also write ahead for permit information. Most park trails are well defined and well marked. They offer backpackers ready—if not easy —access to some of the East's finest wildlands.

If you are hiking the Appalachian Trail from outside the park you can stop at the Twentymile Ranger Station (on the south) or the Big Creek Ranger Station (on the north) to get your permit and reserve shelter space. You can also write ahead for a permit and reservation up to 30 days in advance (see above). For through-hikers— those hiking the entire AT between Maine and Georgia—the situation is different. You can obtain a "through permit" in advance of your trip. Write to Backcountry Permits at the park address and explain your trip.

Because it follows the Smokies crest the AT acts as backbone to a network of trails within the park. With such spur trails, many with their own pleasant waterfall, creek, or other natural feature as an attraction, you have access to the AT from numerous trailheads. Such AT sections are much less crowded than those near Newfound Gap and Clingmans Dome. You get the same sense of walking the crest of eastern America and participating in the trail experience that began as a dream of a pioneering land-use planner, Benton MacKaye, early in this century.

For information about the complete Appalachian Trail write The Appalachian Trail Conference, P.O. Box 236, Harpers Ferry, West Virginia 25425.

Backcountry Basics

While you need a backcountry use permit only for overnight backcountry travel, it would be remiss not to say something about backcountry basics for casual trail walkers and day hikers. Once you leave a parking area or campground in the Smokies, you are in the wilderness. This is the nature of the place. The National Park Service advises against solo camping or hiking in the backcountry. Even experienced hikers can get into trouble and, if alone, may not be able to obtain help. This information is not offered to scare or offend you, but just to make you realize where you are and to make you concerned about your safety.

Stream crossings can be dangerous if the streams are swollen after a rainstorm. Don't attempt to ford a swollen stream. Return to the trailhead and plan another trip. It's worth the extra effort and precaution.

Sudden weather changes are characteristic of the Great Smokies. Be prepared to get wet and either hotter or colder. Rain, wind, and cold can become a deadly combination before you recognize your own symptoms of hypothermia. Rainstorms are typical of warmer weather, so always carry raingear in late spring and summer.

Stay on park trails. If you become lost, do not leave the trail. Particularly, *do not follow a stream* because dense undergrowth will rapidly tire you. Most trails intersect others within a few kilometers and signs at the junctions can put you back on course. If you find yourself lost late in the day, find a protected spot and spend the night. After-dark travel is dangerous. Try to stay warm and dry. Show some sign if possible, such as a fire.

Do not climb on cliff faces and waterfalls. The fine spray mist off waterfalls makes surrounding rocks treacherous footing and increases safety hazards.

If you intend to try winter camping, write to the superintendent for information about the equipment you should have, a backcountry permit, and conditions you may encounter. At higher elevations winter conditions can differ radically from the popular image of winter in the mid-South.

Accommodations

Camping

Camping is a good way to get into the spirit of the Great Smoky Mountains. The National Park Service maintains ten developed campgrounds in the park: at Smokemont, Elkmont, Cades Cove, Cosby, Deep Creek, Look Rock, Balsam Mountain, Cataloochee, Big Creek, and Abrams Creek. Fees are charged. Campgrounds offer water, fireplaces, tables, comfort stations, tent sites, and limited trailer space. No shelters are provided; bring your own and other camping equipment. There are no showers or trailer hookups. Disposal stations for trailer holding tanks are found at Smokemount, Deep Creek, Cades Cove, and Cosby Campgrounds and across the road from the Sugarlands Visitor Center. Primitive campgrounds have pit toilets.

Camping is limited to seven days at all campgrounds during the peak season. You may reserve campsites at Elkmont and Cades Cove in Tennessee and Smokemont in North Carolina by writing to Ticketron Reservations, P.O. Box 617516, Chicago, Illinois 60661-7516. Telephone reservations may be made by calling 1-800-452-1111. For prompt service call the national park (see page 101) for the current per-night camping fee and Ticketron's reservation handling fee. Then mail Ticketron a money order, not a personal check, to cover the reservation plus handling for the entire period you request. **General tips:** Avoid mid-summer's peak camping season. Spring and autumn can be pleasant and offer dazzling flower and leaf-coloration shows. Arrive early in the day and seek your campsite on arrival. Look for a campground off the beaten path, generally away from the Newfound Gap Road (see map).

Chambers of commerce can supply you with commercial camping information. Regional lists of campgrounds are maintained by tourist offices in both Tennessee and North Carolina. For Tennessee write: "Fishing and Camping in East Tennessee," Knoxville Tourist Bureau, 500 Henley St., Knoxville, Tennessee 37901, or telephone (615) 523-2316. For North Carolina write: "North Carolina Outdoors," Travel and Tourism Division, 430 No. Salisbury, Raleigh, North Carolina 27603, or telephone (919) 733-4171.

LeConte Lodge lies atop Mount LeConte, third highest Appalachian peak. You must hike a half-day up mountain trails to get there. Make reservations several months in advance. The lodge sits amidst spruce and fir trees. You can hike in via Alum Caves Bluffs; the lodge sits at trail junctions to Rainbow Falls, Grotto Falls, and the Appalachian Trail. You need bring only personal articles. For information and reservations, write: LeConte Lodge, 250 Lonesome Valley Rd., Sevierville, Tennessee 37862, (615) 429-5704. The only other park accommodations besides campgrounds are the Wonderland Hotel, a small turn-of-the-century hotel in Elkmont. For information or reservations call (615) 436-5490. Closed in winter.

A new breed often encountered on today's trails is called back-packee!

For Your Safety

Bears, Bears, Bears

Tales could be told that would curdle your blood ... but not about the black bear's aggressiveness. These stories would be about the stupidity of some human beings. For reasons of pride in our own species—and so as not to demean bears—we will not recount these tales here. Just this:

The black bear is the largest wild animal in these parts. It can weigh 225 kilograms (500 pounds) or more, but is capable of incredibly fast sprints on rough terrain. It is a wild animal, and protected as such it sometimes loses its normal fear of people. This makes the bear appear tame, but it is then actually more dangerous than its truly wild counterparts. If you come upon a bear while you are in your car, keep the windows shut. Do not attempt to feed, tease, molest, or get close to a bear. Do not try to take a closeup portrait photograph of a bear; either use a telephoto lens or be satisifed with a distant shot.

Avoid and steer clear of a sow bear with cubs. She will do anything to protect them if she thinks they are threatened. Keep in mind that, even if you don't see her, she is seldom far away. Cubs are cute, but you approach or show interest in them at your peril.

Bear feeding is prohibited. It is dangerous to you and those who come after you. It also establishes habits that may lead to the death of the bear. Roadside bears are frequently hit by cars, killed by poachers, or fed harmful substances. Don't be guilty of killing a bear with kindness.

Campers and backpackers must observe certain regulations designed to minimize the extent to which bears are attracted to human pursuits in the park. If you plan to camp or backpack, make sure you are familiar with these regulations on food storage, etc. For example, food cannot be left unattended. If you are backpacking, it must be hung out of reach of bears. If you are camping in a campground, food must be stored in the trunk of your car. Ask for additional information when you obtain your backcountry use permit or when you check into a campground. Failure to observe these regulations may bring a fine.

Theories abound about how to act if you should confront a bear. All such theories assume the bear isn't just as startled as you, and that "bear behavior" is predictable. It is not. As many as 600 bears may inhabit the park. This many individuals of any highly evolved species are unlikely to act—much less to react—with any great predictability.

Hypothermia and Winter Warnings

In the Smokies you must always be prepared for sudden changes in weather, especially as you go from one elevation to another. Know how to take care of yourself in extremes of cold, heat, and wetness. Always carry rain gear because storms arise quickly. In mid-summer at higher elevations a wet hiker can succumb to hypothermia, an all-weather killer. Hypothermia is a condition in which the body loses heat faster than it can generate it. You cannot imagine how rapidly hypothermia symptoms can appear even in mild weather—until they strike you. Then it may be too late. Know how to recognize hypothermia's symptoms: uncontrolled shivering, slurred speech, memory lapse, fumbling hands, stumbling, drowsiness, and inability to get up after a nap.

Prepare yourself against the possibility of hypothermia by keeping a warm, dry layer of clothing next to the body, topped with

a layer to ward off wind and precipitation. Snack often on high-energy foods and take ample liquids. In winter wear multiple layers of insulating clothing under your top layer of rain and wind protection.

Remember that hypothermia strikes in any season, not just winter. Winter hazards include frostbite; icy trails and deep snow; and trails obscured by deep snow.

Management Regulations

Drive safely, observing posted speed limits, and pull off the road or park only at designated areas. Do not leave valuables inside a locked car where they can be seen. Leave them home, take them with you when you leave your car, or lock them in the trunk.

Hunting is prohibited in the park. Firearms must be broken down so they cannot be used. The use of archery equipment, game calls, and spotlights is also prohibited.

All plants, animals, and artifacts are protected by Federal law here. Do not disturb them in any way. Fishing is permitted subject to State and Federal regulation and licensing.

All overnight camping in the backcountry requires a backcountry permit. Otherwise, camp and build fires only in designated campground sites.

A Word About Pets. It is best not to bring pets. They are permitted in the park but only if on a leash or under other physical control at all times. They may not be taken on trails or cross-country hikes. Veterinary services are found in nearby towns. If you want to board your pet during your stay here, check with the chambers of commerce in nearby cities.

There is a saying that high boots will protect you from poisonous snakes, but that common sense is needed to keep you out of trouble with bears. The timber rattlesnake (above) and the copperhead are the only poisonous snakes in these mountains.

Nearby Attractions

To describe the many attractions near the Smokies would require an encyclopedic guidebook. Nearby are TVA's "Great Lakes of the South," Biltmore House and Gardens, large national forests, Oak Ridge's American Museum of Science and Energy, and other features too numerous to mention. Here are just a few features often associated with a Smokies vacation.

The Blue Ridge Parkway has its southern terminus at the North Carolina entrance to the park. This is Craggy Gardens, near Milepost 364, famous for its Catawba rhododendron displays. Several lakes created by Tennessee Valley Authority (TVA) dams provide open water recreation opportunities, including excellent bass fishing, adjacent to or near the park.

The Blue Ridge Parkway. From the northeast the Blue Ridge Parkway makes a delightful highway approach to the Smokies on the North Carolina side. The parkway is administered by the National Park Service and connects Shenandoah National Park, Virginia, with the Great Smoky Mountains National Park. It meticulously follows the southern Appalachians for 755 kilometers (469 miles). It is a roadway designed for motor recreation and so provides leisurely travel free of commercial development. All along it are trails and scenic viewpoints. In season, wildflowers and fall colors can be stupendous. Just before the parkway reaches the Smokies it enters the Balsam Mountains, from which you look directly across at the Smokies. Just after Soco Gap on the parkway you can turn almost due north onto a spur road into the national park's Balsam Mountain Campground and its Heintooga Overlook area.

For a free map and folder detailing services, lodging and accommodations, and points of interest, write: Superintendent, Blue Ridge Parkway, 200 BB and T Building, One Pack Square. Asheville, North Carolina 28801.

The Gateway Cities. For many people a trip to the Smokies is not complete without taking in the sights of Pigeon Forge, Townsend, and/or Gatlinburg, Tennessee,

or Bryson City or Cherokee, North Carolina. At either end of U.S. 441 these municipalities go all-out to serve the tourist trade. Restaurants and motels are major industries along with curio shops, art galleries, and the theme villages that characterize our American tourist scene.

Taken together these surrounding municipalities offer most facilities and services you might need during your stay in the Smokies. Cameras and photographic supplies, groceries, pharmacies, local literature and guides, banks, and countless other services are available.

Cherokee Indian Heritage. The Cherokee Indian Reservation abuts the park boundary on the southeast. In Cherokee there are museums and shops where the art and crafts of these eastern woodlands Indians, thought to be of original Iroquoian stock, are displayed and offered for sale. Each year a play, "Unto These Hills," is performed locally. It describes the Cherokee's history and early encounters with Europeans. Most of these activities occur on the North Carolina side of the park.

Mountain Folkways and Crafts. Mountain ingenuity and the human bent for creativity gave rise to crafts characteristic of the southern mountains. These are kept alive in various outlets surrounding the Smokies. In Gatlinburg you can visit the famed Arrowmont School of Arts and Crafts, which has done so much to revive original handicraft arts and support the artists by marketing their work.

Three main types of basketry are made by Cherokees. Rivercane baskets are now relatively scarce because the once-abundant cane is itself scarce now. White oak baskets are more common. Baskets are also woven from honeysuckle. Above are exquisite examples of basketry by Carol S. Welch, a member of the Eastern Band of Cherokee Indians. The American Museum of Science and Technology at Oak Ridge National Laboratories provides a thoroughly modern contrast to the traditional folkways of the Smokies.

124

Armchair Explorations

Some Books You May Want to Read

The Great Smoky Mountains and their national park are both rich in lore, much of which has been collected and committed to print over the years. Your appreciation of a trip to these mountains can be greatly enhanced, both before and after, by reading accounts of the area's history, natural history, and folklore. There are also field identification guides to nearly everything you see here, from rocks and flowers to spiders and mammals. And there are trail and hiking guidebooks full of good tips and advice on interesting trips, both day trips and overnights. Listed here are selected titles usually available for purchase at park visitor centers, or to be found in your public library. Many of these may also be purchased in bookstores in communities near the park. Several interesting and useful maps of the area are also available. For a more complete list of publications write to the Great Smoky Mountains Natural History Association, Gatlinburg, Tennessee 37738. This non-profit association maintains a sales list of technical and other books about the Smokies as part of its efforts to enhance the interpretation of the park's values to the public.

Brooks, Maurice. *The Appalachians,* Houghton Mifflin Company, 1965.

Broome, Harvey. *Out Under the Sky of the Great Smokies,* The Greenbrier Press, 1975.

Campbell, Carlos. *Birth of a National Park in the Great Smoky Mountains,* The University of Tennessee Press, 1960.

Cantu, Rita. *Great Smoky Mountains:* *The Story Behind the Scenery,* KC Publications, 1979.

Dykeman, Wilma and Jim Stokely. *At Home in the Smokies,* National Park Service Handbook 125, 1978.

Frome, Michael. *Strangers in High Places: The Story of the Great Smoky Mountains,* The University of Tennessee Press, 1980.

Kephart, Horace. *Our Southern Highlanders,* The University of Tennessee Press, 1922.

Shields, Randolph. *The Cades Cove Story,* Great Smoky Mountains Natural History Association, 1977.

Tilden, Freeman. *The National Parks,* Alfred A. Knopf, 1968.

Index

Numbers in italics refer to photographs, illustrations, or maps.

☆ GPO: 1981 — 341-611/7
Reprint 1991

...ational Park Service

The National Park Service expresses its appreciation
to all those persons who made the preparation and production of this handbook possible. The Service also
gratefully acknowledges the financial support given this
handbook project by the Great Smoky Mountains Natural
History Association, a nonprofit group that assists interpretive efforts at Great Smoky Mountains National Park.

Illustrations
All photographs and other artwork not credited below
are from the files of the Great Smoky Mountains
National Park and the National Park Service.
American Museum of Science and Energy, 124
museum.
William A. Bake   covers, 6, 10-11, 33 trillium, 35
yellow-poplar and mushrooms, 45, 52, 58, 59 bird's-foot
violet, 61 mountain laurel, 66, 78, 92 farmer, 93
hen. 123 Blue Ridge Parkway.
Greg Beaumont   62 except turkey, 63 opossum.
Ed Cooper   4-5, 12-13, 18-19, 34, 38, 92-93 buildings,
100.
Edouard E. Exline   85, 86 coopering, 88 hide and
staves, 89 shaping metal, 91 ginning.
Daniel Feaser   44 fish.
George Founds   74, 76.
Charles S. Grossman   86 tub mill, 87 rolling cane,
89 gunsmithing, 91 churning, carding and washday.
Joseph S. Hall   47 angler.
Indian Arts and Crafts Board   97 baskets, 124 baskets.
Royce Jenkins   46 yellow hammer and yellow wooly
worm.
John MacGregor   64-65 except rattlesnake, pine snake,
and red-cheeked salamander.
Kenneth McDonald   14-15, 20, 22-23, 24, 37 sundew,
98-99, 112 angler, 114, 115 tenter, 116, 119, 122 boat.
Steve Moore   46 except Jenkins, 47 fly.
Alan Rinehart   87 mill interior, hauling wood, and
splitting shingles, 89 basketry.
Smithsonian Institution   96.
Laura Thornborough   90, 91 baskets.